The Story of Helena

LOVE

D

First published in Great Britain in 1975 by
MAYHEW-McCRIMMON LTD
Great Wakering Essex

First reprint: July 1976
Second reprint: January 1978

ISBN 0-85597-084-7

Printed by Mayhew-McCrimmon Ltd.

This book is dedicated to Willeke,
Helena's beloved Mummy.

ACKNOWLEDGEMENT

The title "Love and Let Go" was inspired by the profound and beautiful poem "Walking Away" by C. Day Lewis. The author heard it read on the radio by Jill Balcon and imperfectly remembered the last line which rightly reads:–

"And love is proved in the letting go".

The author is in debt to both C. Day Lewis for his wisdom and to Mrs. J. Day Lewis for allowing him to misquote.

It is not growing like a tree
In bulk, doth make man better be;
Or standing long, an oak, three hundred year,
To fall a log at last, dry, bald and sere;
A lily of a day
Is fairer far in May,
Although it fall and die that night
It was the plant and flower of Light.
In small proportions we just beauties see;
And in short measures life may perfect be.

Ben Jonson

The Harbinger

There was a clear precision about the afternoon. The sun was high, the sky incredibly clear, the straight road shone like a river. From the grass verge ventured a stoat and her family of five, their long lithe bodies rippling like a tawny serpent. A car rushed up the hill, it was upon them, the tawny group delayed a moment, regained valour and rippled on to the far verge: the mother turning saw her fifth child move, shudder, drop and darted back to her dying child, paused, then returned to the living. But she did pause.

1

SCARBOROUGH

"The glory and freshness of a dream".

William Wordsworth

The band would play interminable fox-trots, so we left the ballroom. This evening on our holiday in my home-town of Scarborough, was proving a disappointment. The ballroom itself had shrunk as places remembered from childhood and revisited so often do. The vast joyous cavern of my ninth and tenth years at Peter Cornish's Christmas parties turned out to be only an average room for a hotel of its size and certainly to me in my mood of disenchantment lacking in the magical element that I had endowed it in my memory. I had expected much much more.

So leaving the band to its out-of-date syncopations, – we were after all in the Rock and Roll age,– we went down the corridor to the hall. Here, I knew, we should find that particular charm of Second Empire, elegance, good proportions but with sudden surprising curves, a baroque that was more opulent than playful. It was all white and gold and crimson, gay but formal. This was better than I had remembered; my spirits rose and as we climbed the central staircase, which then branched left and right, I told Willeke, my wife, as she lifted her long white dress with its pattern of big pink roses, that this was the very spot where Peter Cornish and I had been chased by the porter.

On the first landing I showed her where it was possible to hide behind a pillar and flick paper pellets over the balustrade at the head of the hall porter on duty at his counter. A delight made even more delightful because his well-trained countenance never flickered though struck again and again and again as he busied himself with keys. Now my heart really did begin to soar for all I saw was far superior to my memories : I did not remember this buhl cabinet, this table inlaid with coloured marbles, these scrolled and delicate writing desks. A person of very distinguished taste had been here.

Then suddenly we came upon the Empress Eugenie in the central bay of the landing. It was Winterhalter's state portrait and very calmly she surveyed me from behind that perfectly oval face through her almond shaped eyes; her left hand about to twitch her train; her right hand indicated a crown with, it seemed, a demure surprise. I had not thought of the Empress for twenty years.

I led Willeke up more passages, more staircases and at every turn there was a picture, here a Landseer, there a Turner, just beyond a Rossetti, nearby a Burne-Jones. We were enraptured, it was such an unexpected bonus in an hotel, and for me it was something I understood far better than the intricacies of the fox-trot which I had never mastered.

I forgot my lack of prowess and disappointment and slowly we trailed back from picture to picture quite forgetting the lateness of the hour and only realising it as a door opened and a military looking gentleman, in a dressing gown, glared at us, then squared his shoulders and marched resolutely to the lavatory.

Then another door opened more shyly and an elderly lady with her hair hanging in a thin plait, clutching a toilet bag, hesitated then smiled and as she passed said "They are lovely, aren't they?" and passed on rather self-consciously.

We wandered on and on, but I stopped to have another look at the Empress. Her magnificence amazed me and I wondered where the portrait had hung since it left Winterhalter's atelier : an Embassy, or in the office of some self-important consul in a manufacturing city? I rejoiced that, now, she presided – no, reigned here; and that her matchless taste had inspired the interior decorator. For I now noticed that all the colours lavished on the staircase and landings – white, crimson and gold –

had their origin in the picture.

To return to the ballroom would have been an anti-climax. After all we had seen one could dance only to Strauss, Waldteufel and Offenbach, so we decided to leave. The stars shone very bright in the sky and the salt air blew in very gently from the sea of the great bay of Scarborough. There were lights around the trim flower beds of the Town Hall which were grouped, as I had always remembered them, around the plinth of the statue of dumpy, grumpy Queen Victoria. A personage whom, nevertheless, I had loved ever since I was four and had stood near her statue as my mother was selling Remembrance day poppies.

We walked back to our old car and as we crossed the Valley Bridge to the South Cliff we saw the moon sinking behind the cenotaph on Oliver's Mount. At Greylands we crept in closing the front door very gently on its well-oiled hinges, quite needlessly, for my cousin Sybil though in bed was wide awake. She was reading a book by Gerald Vann on Sacrifice, hard going I would have thought at two in the morning. We noticed that she laid theology aside quite happily to hear of our more worldly adventures of the evening.

My cousin's home had been that of her parents; when my great uncle had died she had divided it into three flats, but it still remained a spacious place. The bedroom assigned to us had once been the dining room and I could recall many portentous meals there, surrounded by very heavy mahogany and a very sepia wallpaper. It was now transformed; the brown had been ousted by pink; and my great-aunt's Edwardian satinwood furniture brought down, so that it had an ample feminine turn-of-the-century gaiety.

I remember this holiday so well because it was a very significant one, it marked the end of four years of hard work and strain for us both. When Willeke and I had been married in the Hague on 4th September 1954, eight months after I had been ordained and three months after Willeke had qualified as a medical doctor at Leiden University, we had returned to the parish of Hales Owen, an industrial town on the edge of the Black Country.

The first months of our marriage had been full of difficulties, partly financial – we were desperately poor – but also emotional. Within weeks of our honeymoon Willeke discovered herself to be pregnant; and at the same time we realised that my mother, living in Winchester, was dying of cancer. The Winter of 1955 was bleak; but the Spring was still bleaker for on May 30th, after an illness of agonizing pain, my mother died in our little house in Hales Owen. She was cremated on the afternoon of June 1st and in the early hours of June 2nd our daughter, Diana, had been born.

Whilst Diana was still in her cradle, still on a bottle, Willeke enrolled at Birmingham University and recommenced life as a medical student, for her Dutch degree could not be registered with the General Medical Council. So, very bravely, she started to work for a British qualification, doing ward rounds. Her life was very complicated, rushing off to the Queen Elizabeth Hospital and back, to see if Diana was alright, reading her books and at the same time discovering all the manifold complexities of being a parson's wife.

I, with a year's start on her, had not yet plumbed all the shallows and depths of life in a parish with its many strains and utterly divergent stresses and demands. It is a strange life and one that no author, certainly in the present day, has adequately described in any literary form.

Four very rewarding years were spent in Hales Owen and then we moved to Bewdley, where we were parted for six months whilst Willeke did a house job at Kidderminster Hospital. That was a very trying time because the parish failed to get the accommodation they had promised us, so Diana and I were for a time homeless as well. But eventually we did get a little house which we loved dearly. So when Willeke went to Ronkswood Hospital for the next six months there were often difficulties but it was not quite so hard. It was to celebrate the end of this six months that we were on holiday in Scarborough.

However, it was not of these months that I was thinking as I lay in bed: it was of my wife's beauty. In my mind's eye I saw her lifting her long white dress to climb the curved stairs of the hotel, as she had done an hour or two before. In the darkness I recalled her decisive movements, her glowing youth. Suddenly behind her I saw another beauty, the Empress Eugenie; and in the strange joy of creation I saw not just the picture of studied calm and poise, but so revealingly I saw the Empress move. Only then did I know the full secret of that woman's charm.

That night a child was conceived.

The journey back to Worcestershire was devious, by way of the Dales and Haworth. The Parsonage had been newly decorated, but it was too pretty, too colourful, it was even playful: it had been drabber, more serviceable and parasitically enduring in the Brontes day. Yet still the intensity of those women lingered there and looking out of the upstairs window over the churchyard we decided to go home straight away. So back we hurried to our dark and damp little house, built largely of wattle and daub between its vast timbers. Many might condemn it as inconvenient, but to us it was home, the very spirit of it, warm and cosy, as it had been to many families over its four centuries of life.

2
WAITING

"The thought of our past years in me doth breed
Perpetual benedictions." *William Wordsworth*

The pregnancy seemed long and Willeke often was totally exhausted and her face sharpened in all its contours. My cousin Dawn and her husband Don invited us to join them on a trip in their old car to St. Tropez and encouraged by Gaston Harward, my Rector, we went. It was a long hot and crushed journey and we read – it seemed a thousand times – the story of Epaminondas and his mother's umbrella to Diana. We camped at little villages, putting up our ancient tents with their guy ropes next to the sophisticated canvas dwellings of the French, who, arriving after us, would be preparing their dinner on camping-gaz, Madame in a spotless housecoat, whilst we were still crawling around with mallets and pumping away at temperamental primus stoves.

At St. Tropez we were welcomed to a neat clean little hotel and by luck stumbled, the first evening, on a wonderful restaurant, away from the quayside, where I learnt that good food is an art to be appreciated. It was run by *le patron;* his charming wife would circulate amongst the tables to see that the clientele were enjoying themselves; and their daughter waited. Willeke, Dawn and I thought the daughter was the most beautiful woman we had ever seen – tall, slim, dark unmistakeably Gallic, but with a profile straight from Ancient Greece, She moved with an air of unapproachable aloofness, even grandeur; however, this immense pride did not make her contemptuous of her task, as it might an Englishwoman, but even more efficient and thoughtful. As I delighted in the food I wondered whether my son, Alexander, would enjoy good food as well?

There were many other enchantments: the market place with its piles of brilliantly coloured fruit and vegetables (there was something of Gauguin in the textures and the colours); the sensual shape of all those heaps of grapes the size of damsons; peaches as golden as Jaffas; green figs splitting to reveal their maroon flesh like an Elizabethan slashed doublet. The year was 1958 and the housewife, just as in the picture of my old French text book, was still followed by her bonne with the basket.

In snorkels, which I had been lent, I discovered the pale gold world of the undersea, I spent hours plunging, gazing, surfacing around the rocks of la Cote des Maures. On the lilo I took Diana on long voyages, once staying out for two hours and finding a very anxious Willeke on shore when we glided back very pleased with ourselves.

On our return journey we left Don and Dawn in Paris and we continued on to Holland to see Willeke's parents in the Hague. I shall always remember Dawn, who is younger than either of us, becoming very maternal on the platform of Gare du Nord, and gazing into Willeke's tired face and saying "Are you sure you will be alright?" After seeing our Dutch relatives we returned to England and Dawn with the same concern written on her face met us at Liverpool Street Station.

As I look back on my wife's three pregnancies I can see, so clearly, that our activities, our prevailing moods and our circumstances in those months have had a significant effect upon the character of the unborn child. When Diana was being carried, her pre-natal growth was completely overshadowed by my mother's fatal illness. It would seem that our preoccupation and our necessary control over ourselves at that time gave her a kind of calm maturity. She has always been a very reasonable, steadfast and capable child.

Laura, our youngest, had a very peaceful growth : we had been secure in a country parish, and life, though busy, had been unhurried. As a result she is a peaceful, unhurried and thoughtful child.

Helena's gestation was nomadic, very sociable and very busy. So her character is enquiring, zestful for new people and places.

Mothers have often told me how their children were born with their characters. I have found it so; therefore I cannot regard abortion as anything other than a kind of murder.

As Christmas drew near Willeke realized that she must have a dress for occasions, so she cut up and adapted her silk anthracite dress. It was a dress we had bought together during our engagement for a Gala performance of "King Lear" by the Old Vic Company in the Hague. Refashioned, it now covered her vast size; and I recall her moving majestically and with a pretty face once more amongst a crowd at Ribbesford House at a cocktail party.

The people of Bewdley took the greatest interest in the forthcoming child. As I visited, as I went shopping, there would be enquiries about my wife; and always then came the half question "I expect you want a boy?" There were assurances that it would be, for "You see she is carrying it so high." Another week and the question was "Are there any twins in your family?" "Yes, as a matter of fact, my wife is a twin." "There now, what did I say? You'll certainly have twins."

At one point even Dr David Sargent thought there might be twins. It was all very exciting and few babies were more eagerly awaited.

February came cold; in the parish I was busy; and to add to the problems of the Rector and myself, Bewdley was flooded. One Sunday night he knocked on our door and said, "Come and see the river." So Gaston, Joan, Willeke and I went down to the bridge, Telford's, and there one could feel the might of the waters swirling down from Wales and Shropshire and thudding and drumming against the piers. It was exhilarating, exciting but also a little frightening.

Willeke felt much better, her energy returned and on the fifteenth she walked up to wish Miss Whitcombe a happy birthday; it was her hundred and second. They sat happily by the fire and the old lady told Willeke of her interview with Florence Nightingale, whom she called Miss Nightingale, before being taken on as a probationer at St. Thomas's Hospital. She admired Diana's dress, "So much nicer than those brown Holland dresses we had made each year. I hated them."

"But surely", said her niece, "it did not matter for you all had those nice white pinafores with goffering."

"White pinafores! They did not come in until I was grown up, my dear."

That night, while Diana was asleep in bed, we sat by the fire choosing names. Willeke was very good, she always let me choose them, but gave herself the right to veto. It was still to be Alexander for a boy and Helena Victoria for a girl. Both stemmed from my first year at university. In Ancient History I had been fascinated by the career of Alexander the Great and Helena because of those splendid lines of Marlowe:

> Sweet Helen, make me immortal with a kiss:
> Her lips suck forth my soul, see where it flies;
> Come Helen, come give me my soul again.
> Here will I dwell, for heaven be in those lips,
> And all is dross that is not Helena.

How well I remember coming upon those lines for the first time in the old library beneath the great window at Lampeter.

Victoria, just because I like the Queen, the period, and the name. Together, because they run together like a gentle but bright brook, decorous, but friendly.

As I sat on the floor gazing into the fire, dreaming, Willeke rose, "I'll make some cocoa."

I stared on full of imaginings when suddenly I realized she had been gone at least twenty minutes. I went through the little dining room to the kitchen and there was Willeke crouched in the middle of the room. There was something primitive, elemental about her posture, I was horribly afraid.

"What shall I do? What shall I do?" I cried.

The reply was so prosaic, so ludicrous that my panic vanished in laughter, "Stoke the Rayburn." Which I did.

Then I wrapped up Willeke, ran upstairs for the case, ready packed, but only that afternoon, and flew down the High Street for the car at the Rectory. It was powdering with snow, I slipped on some ice but righted myself, ran on and prayed that the very temperamental car would start. It did. Sitting behind the steering wheel I felt the drama of the occasion as I saw the pink light glow through the Rectory's drawing room curtains; there in contrast sat quietly Gaston and Joan. Back at the house, Willeke seemed to have shrunk; she seemed almost frightened.

We drove gingerly over the icy roads to Kidderminster. The Maternity home was brilliantly lit and a couple of nurses took Willeke in and I was dismissed. Back at home Diana still slept peacefully. I rang up Dr Sargent and told him that Willeke was in the home and then I went to bed.

I slept soundly and was wakened by Diana who demanded "Where's Mummy?" I dressed her, got breakfast, took her to Load Street to be picked up by her teacher to go to school and returned home. As I entered, the telephone rang. Answering it I heard a friendly voice saying, "There's a fine husband! I have sleepless night delivering your baby and I cannot wake you with the telephone ringing five solid minutes. You have another little girl."

Only momentarily did my heart sink for I had wanted an Alexander. I thanked the doctor, put down the receiver and instantly thought, "How delightful, I really have a Helena."

At eleven I went to the Maternity Home. Willeke looked pink and flushed and excited. Her room was already bursting into bloom. I was taken by a nurse to see my new daughter. She was surprisingly small – she had made her mother so large. She was dark and fast asleep after the trauma of birth.

The room was lit by the reflected light from the snow on the ground, there were no shadows on the ceiling and in this clearness I had a kind of clairvoyance. I wrote in my diary, "I had a vision of a difficult life ahead of this minute sleeping person. God avert that vision, or at least modify it." As I wrote it I knew that I was expressing myself very badly. However, I was trying to put into words something inexpressible. I cannot, even now, say what caused that feeling, nor could I define the difficulties I seemed to foresee. I do know, though, that I returned to Bewdley very disquieted.

Next day Willeke suffered reaction and was very sleepy and on the Thursday I took Diana to see her mother and her sister. It was very charming to see Diana take Helena with great tenderness and even greater awe upon her knee. This baby on a second viewing was so neat, I rightly foresaw that she would be pretty, but wrongly that she would be of a pinker complexion than Diana : for Helena became above all "pale and proud". That night as Diana said her prayers she mentioned Helena for the first time amongst her "God blesses" but when she ended she demanded querulously, "Why did God send a iittle girl when he knew I wanted a boy?"

3

THE BABY

"A wish and a prayer and . . . . . . "

Another week went by and I brought Willeke and Helena home. When I had them both by the fire of the sitting room of the little Tudor House I saw how very weak Willeke was and how tiny and frail Helena: I was quite alarmed.

From that hour the house seemed full of baby trappings, washing, nappies, rattles, a pram and tins of National Dried Milk. Yet, strangely, I loved it all; it spoke of life unending, ages yet to come, new adventures and new discoveries that were for me as well. I knew so many houses so different, – perfect but sterile, where even if things bloomed they never came to fruition. I knew, too, houses that spoke only of the past and resolutely ignored the future. I knew houses where there was neither pride in the past, nor hope in the future.

The weakness of Willeke persisted and I telephoned Val-Ann, my cousin, and asked her to come for the weekend to help us; which she did very efficiently and also brought us news of London. When she had gone Willeke remained housebound, for the weather was dark and cold. The first outing that Helena had was next door, to the Verger and his wife: we shared the yard – once the pump had been shared as well. Mrs. Layton, always a good neighbour, welcomed them effusively and to our amazement pressed into Helena's one palm a silver florin and into the other a shining piece of coal that she had scrubbed. "I am from Durham," she explained, "and that means that she will never lack money and never be cold." It came true.

Our first baby had been easy and contented, taking her milk, sleeping well and right through the night. It was something of a shock to us that Helena did not repeat this pattern. She drank very slowly, was frequently sick and woke for these lengthy feeds at regular four hourly intervals by day and by night.

It was now my turn to visit Miss Whitcombe. She was rather blind so did not recognise me. But when she realized who it was she jumped to her feet to grasp my hand and congratulate me.

"And what shall you call her?"

"Helena Victoria."

"I am very fond of the name Helena and Victoria, of course, after our good Queen."

I could but smile, the emphasis on good was so pronounced that all subsequent queens it implied were bad. I asked the old lady if she had ever seen Queen Victoria.

"No. But when I was four we all went to Cowes. My father had been told that the Queen and the Prince would drive out from Osborne that afternoon. Mother made us practise curtseys all morning. We went to the Lodge and waited and waited. They had left by another drive. So I never saw her."

I worked it out, it must have been the summer of 1861 before the Prince Consort died. I stored that tale for Helena to tell her grandchildren.

Those early days of Helena I remember only partially because I am not terribly fond of babies also, at that time, I was very preoccupied wondering what kind of parish I would be given as my first living. I wasted a lot of time on this, letting the present slip by.

The preoccupation soon had grist for the mill: the Bishop of Worcester offered me the parish of Great Witley with its magnificent baroque church, the finest of its kind in Britain. I accepted the living for I loved the church and I liked the two churchwardens immediately on sight. There was, however, a big disappointment; we would have to live in a small modern rectory, which was half-built. That was a blow to which I never was able to reconcile myself for I had always dreamt of a large

Vicarage.

On April 22nd Diana and I went into the lovely Wyre Forest, which borders Bewdley and from which in the past Bewdley derived most of its wealth. It was a place that I knew well and we were able to go unhesitatingly to the banks facing south for primroses and violets; to the marshes by Dowles Brook for kingcups and in the meadow, just above Wyre Forest Halt, there were the first cowslips. From the woodland itself, last of all so they would not droop, we picked my favourite flower, the wind flower or wood anemone. When Diana was in bed Willeke and I went down to Ribbesford Church and arranged this wreath of flowers about the font. When finished it looked exquisite and would have sent the Victorian diarist Francis Kilvert into rhapsodies. That night I wrote in my diary, "I hope that Helena grows up to have the beauty of a wood anemone, pale, slender, very very fine and delicate – yet definite in outline and structure. Pure beauty."

I had all that I wished for but also a little more.

Helena's godparents were two old friends and a new one. There was Elizabeth Hackett from Hales Owen whom we had seen grow up, the other godmother was Elizabeth Godwin whom we had met in Bewdley and loved immediately. Richard Bevan, who had been at Queen's Theological College in Birmingham with me, was godfather. The service was the new one then current and at the service Liz Godwin produced Helena's gift, a silver candlestick to hold her baptismal candle. It was a bright happy April day when the finest place to be, as poets often tell, is England and particularly the countryside. The Harwards had given us the use of the Rectory and people wandered in and out of the large drawing room through the vast sash windows.

There was another movement afoot at this stage: a locum priest was needed in Stornoway in the Outer Hebrides. Again with the aid of the Rector, who really did spoil me, I wrote for it. It was very good of him to be so helpful for the Parish Fete came in the middle of the period when I would be away. His reaction had been, "Not go to the Outer Hebrides because of a fete! My dear

David, you will have more than enough of those awful affairs in your lifetime, miss any you can is my advice."

We left in June staying at Shap, then in Edinburgh and lastly in a cottage in Fort William. The last tiny cottage I remember well and especially the capped and gowned sons and daughters who looking down on us from the wall earnestly grasping their degrees whilst we equally earnestly grasped our knives and forks. It was only at the end of the journey, half an hour before landing in Stornoway that I regretted the undertaking: Willeke was succumbing to sea-sickness and the children were so tired. In the house, though, I wrote "Diana has been very good indeed, Helena angelic and the journey has been a joy most of the time."

It was an almost perfect holiday. Willeke's twin sister joined us and later Richard, Helena's godfather. The strange atmosphere of the island enchanted us; there was a quality of timelessness everywhere – not just in shops and daily contacts where there was no bustle and no hurry – but in the moors, the treeless wastes, the little islands off-shore.

Willeke kept saying "It's like the beginning of the world." Helena went everywhere with us, to the beaches, into the terrifying dry-stone wall tower of the Doune of Carloway, where once an entire clan was burnt alive; across the fields to the deserted but well-kept church of Rodil; one day she lay like a tiny human sacrifice in the midst of the stones of Callanish whilst we older ones chased one another in and out of the pillars.

The magical quality of the isles was crystallized for me when we went to the Mod, what the Welsh would call an Eisteddfod. In the usual gaunt hall was a stage and a piano. There groups or individuals would climb up and sing or play. Most were very good indeed.

Immediately before us sat two young men, one looked pitifully thin and shrunken and had so yellow a pallor and such thick black hair I thought him an oriental. Twice a name was called and the guinea-coloured young man was then pushed to his feet by his friend. He shambled to the stage, his ill-fitting best suit awkwardly accompanying him seemingly equally reluctant of its own free-will. He then faced the audience, his face turned from yellow to green, a note on the piano was struck, he cocked his head to one side and sang: it seemed with his right ear lifted upwards he was listening to a heavenly sound that he was merely relaying to us. It was mystical sound like nothing I have ever heard since. He cast a spell upon the whole hall, everyone listened alert, intent, alive. He ended and the greatest compliment an artist can be given was awarded him, a pause of absolute silence before an absolute roar of applause. The adjudicator remained still, then said, obviously moved, "Could you sing it to us again?"

Colour flowed into his face, he smiled, again he cocked his head over his left shoulder and once more this transcendent melody flowed out. Pleased but shy he left the stage amidst even louder applause. I felt a thrill of pride that such a man sat by me; he was a wizard. In fact, I expect, he was a weaver: he looked a loner and I imagine he sang in just that way as he worked at his loom. At the end of the evening his name was called again and again, he was the laureate of the day, but he was nowhere to be found.

Willeke and I wandered back to our temporary home gazing out at the sea which was so still, so calm and so light. It was nearly eleven but still old ladies in straw hats were making social calls. However we could not linger unduly: Helena called; her timetable did not vary. It was here in Stornoway I came to know her, for she demanded her first feed at six, then she would lie on the white expanse of the bed beside me kicking and laughing.

4

NEW HOME

"We'll talk of sunshine and of song:
And summer days when we were young."

William Wordsworth

After all the inevitable delays in the building of a house, we moved to Great Witley; the date was November 1960. It was a great event for us all but not without its problems. We moved from the close community of a small town with houses huddled together and many callers to a house aloof in a field where no one called. I well remember how delighted we were near Christmas when Mr and Mrs Cotton just dropped in to see us. From this experience I can understand how slum dwellers, after a lifetime of cosy squalor, find adjustment to new surroundings very difficult.

To Diana the move meant also a new school as well as a new home.

Helena, we suppose, never realized the change; she was only eight months. She herself was changing, her dark hair was being replaced by some much finer and fairer on a head that was exceptionally round and neat. Willeke called her "my Cupid" and indeed there was something of a Meissen cherub about her. Her skin was smooth, indeed flawless, but if she had a ceramic quality, it was very much Meredith's "rogue in porcelain." As she grew in agility, she grew in mischief and crawling around she left a trail of havoc. Workbaskets were her especial delight: in her hands knitting left its needles. I was very angry when she tore out the title pages of some of the volumes of Fanny Burney's Diary – "War and Peace" has pages missing still. However, an even greater sin was that she would make off with the post, leaving a trail of envelopes partially chewed or torn.

It was at this time that I was one day awaiting a party of visitors to the splendid Parish Church: they were late, so I beguiled the time by glancing through the Visitor's Book. One very squiggly, very baroque signature interested me, it was Sacheverell Sitwell's. I was very pleased, but not surprised, that so illustrious a connoisseur of the eighteenth century should have visited us. His visit coincided with the planning of a new guide book and immediately I thought who would be better to write us a really good introduction. I wrote to him and then waited week after week for a reply. As time passed I grew very disappointed that there was no response, even if it was only to say "No." I gave up hope, but was surprised that a Sitwell should be so discourteous. Then one morning, Willeke exclaimed, "Why, here's a letter for you. I found it under the mattress of the carry-cot." It was more than a month old and it was a most charming and decisive assent to my request. I, now, had to write to Mr. Sitwell and explain why I had not replied. In all our subsequent letters he never failed to send his love to Helena.

Soon she was a toddler, a mixture of gaiety – tremendous gaiety – and the utmost seriousness. At one moment daring and adventurous and dashing with heavy lists to one side or the other as she rushed from chair to table, or up the stairs, yet she feared to walk without any handy support for a long time. She loved new things, new places but was revolted by new foods and when encountering new faces could adopt a marmoreal countenance that never left her. She was a bewildering mixture. In my diary I contrasted her with her cousin Katherine Ann who was two months younger, but always slightly taller than Helena, superficially they seemed alike in temperament, however I noted, "Katherine has an elfin charm with her dark complexion and deep set eyes and pointed chin; she seems a child of this age. Helena has full eyes and a roundness of face, plus a stillness and repose that seem of another century."

Just before her first birthday she said "Daddy" and "Diana", both easy sounds involving only the tongue and the teeth, but "Mummy" never came. It is, of course a more labial and complicated a noise, yet even so Helena was late in achieving it and the one she so obviously adored was her mother. Any day we expected it in the hubble-bubble of noise: at one meal as she gazed lovingly at Willeke we awaited for "Mummy" to emerge, but no, instead very distinctly came "Helena" which so shocked her that she squirmed with embarrassment. She was so sweet and also so vehement and I regarded her with even more concern after the mother of my first Rector came to see us. I had long known her in Winchester, Mega Blakiston, charming and wise. As we talked and we had so much in common to discuss I said, "Isn't it fascinating to see oneself appear in one's children."

She looked at me with a very sybilline eye and replied, "I often found it horrifying and very humiliating." The bubble of my self-esteem was pricked, yes, perhaps it was more humiliating than fascinating and I watched Helena with a more apprehensive regard. Always, though, I ended up fascinated, for there was so much that was me, but equally there was herself and herself alone and that self was a charmer.

Her first birthday came on the sixteenth of February 1961. To celebrate it we had our neighbour Mrs Treadwell aged 88 years and her daughter Dorothy in to tea. Mrs Treadwell was a woman of indefatigable vitality and consummate beguilement; she and Helena had an immediate affection for one another. In the light of the solitary candle on the cake they beamed at one another with the brightest of eyes. It was left, though, to big sister Diana to blow out the candle.

Diana was by now reconciled to Helena, though her displeasure at receiving a sister had not abated, but rather intensified and so annoyed was she by her sex that she decreed herself a little boy and would answer only to the name of Tommy. She was not maternally inclined and was often missing when Helena was bathed and put to bed and the four and a half years' gap never seemed to lessen, they were two quite separate children.

It was now that a year began that I do not recall very well. It was a year in which I was often unwell and a time when Helena cried a very great deal; the *daimon* of her personality gave her no peace and none for her parents either; it was her intensity of spirit revealing itself. She was ambitious to do things far beyond her capabilities and when she failed to achieve them she was considerably irritated at her own inability. She was angered in the extreme when we took her from her self-appointed tasks to eat meals, or change clothes and go out and we found that her will was very strong. Like all small girls she loved water and mud. Her first visit to the seaside, Tenby, was a stupendous revelation. At first she regarded the waves with suspicion, quelled her fear and then rushed in and out with incredulous delight. Water: masses and masses of it; and an infinity of sand and wonder of wonders, parents pleased when she played and played in it.

A parson spends so much of his time in his home, that for him to have the correct type of house is of an importance that cannot be overestimated. The Church Commissioners and the Diocesan architects have this at heart; but financial factors always have to be considered; the whims of fashion also prevail. So mistakes are made. The modern house in Witley proved inadequate in every way for a young family, the open plan of the drawing room and the dining room was a bugbear. It meant there was no room we could turn over to the children and say, "That is yours, treat it how you will." We spent so much time tidying up and disliking ourselves for doing so for it seemed we were repressing the children.

Yet, I know, as I write this, that compared with thousands we were lucky, yet we were human and so tended to envy our colleagues who had larger and better houses than our own and they, so often, were so vociferous in their condolences to us that they did not help. The house was noisy, too, the hollow doors echoed reverberatingly when banged and the walls were thin. So when the old Police Station was demolished I went down and bought a lorry load of bricks, the splendid Gothic door, and four lattice paned windows and built myself, with some aid, a gazebo where I could work undisturbed. A very perceptive parishioner said when she saw it. "That is a manifestation of the hermit in you." She was very right.

At this time I had a sense of failure towards Helena: I was not sufficiently patient and I was very pre-occupied with the parish. Like many many parents I longed and longed for the next stage of Helena's development. Willeke often said, "It's only a phase". I agreed it was, but still I wanted improvement. At times I was so pained by her behaviour that I wondered if she really was our child and wondered if the Maternity Home had muddled the babies. I could not believe that anyone in my family could be so aggressive, so demanding. I looked, of course, only at the gentle ones for my comparison and never, never at myself.

"Why, oh, why was she so different to Diana?" This I asked myself again and again and then a friend much more interested in psychology than I, explained that the second child is not born into the same environment as the first, he, or she, arrives into a world composed not of two, but three and one of those is a rival for the affection of the parents. "Helena", he said, "was born into a competitive world; she feels that she must vie with Diana for your love." Scales fell from my eyes: it was true, terribly true. Helena was so like me; but Fate had decreed that she have a sister; I was an only child. Like me she would have rejoiced in the role of the only one, I felt very sorry for her; again I was wrong, for the soul only grows as it conquers and she fought a fight with her lesser self with that same intensity that she brought to everything and in a much shorter space of time far outstripped her father.

After the Easter of 1961, John and Shirley Hebditch who lived in the next village, offered to take Diana and Helena for a few days so that Willeke and I could go away without the children, a thing we had never done before. We went to the Dales of Yorkshire feeling very young and very carefree. Nonetheless we were very surprised when a retired couple in the little hotel took us for honeymooners. The husband was also very anxious to discover my profession: he tried first composer, alas, I cannot even read music; university lecturer; and ending up with accountant, well I can add up, but never subtract with accuracy. On the third and last morning at the Red Lion I looked for him, before leaving, to tell him what I really was, but I could not find him anywhere.

It is, I think, very good for clergy to remove their clerical collars, for you suddenly see a side of one's fellows that they usually hide. They restrain their language less. But most of all it is such a relief not to be drowned beneath a mass of churchy talk of the utmost triviality, which laity switch on for, as they think, the benefit of the clergy. And the further they are removed from contact with the church, the more, it seems, they have compulsion to prove a link. I cannot tell how many elderly men have related to me their tales of life as choir boys before the '14-'18 war; and women will tell me of tea cosies they have knitted for bazaars, thirty years ago – and for which the Vicar was not "truly thankful". Alas, for them that it is the sum total of their religious experience, or perhaps I should say church experience. So it means a lot of failure on the part of many people, which includes clergy as well.

Well, every calling has its hazards. My wife likes on holiday to be equally anonymous, for she is a natural prey for the hypochondriacs and as I hear of the enormities of some vicar, so she hears of the equal enormities of the local medical practitioners.

On our return from Yorkshire we drove straight to the Hebditches. Shirley came out into the garden as we arrived, carrying Helena in her arms, instantly as I saw them in the sunlight I knew that both of them had had a very difficult time. Poor Shirley in the clear sunlight, suddenly looked older and Helena was just lost. She held out her arms and shrieked when she saw her beloved Mummy. Swiftly we took her home where she was promptly ill. We learnt, though, how gentle and motherly Diana had been to Helena whilst we were away, so again we learnt of another side of one of our children.

5

GROWING

"Thou child of joy."

William Wordsworth

1962 was the year that Helena's personality crystallized and when our temperaments, so alike, either fused or exploded. It was also a year in which I was very unhappy; the summer was wet, the talk gloomy and whenever we went out to a meal with friends, or parishioners, the discussion always ended with "the bomb". I was so bored with "the bomb". I also felt depressed concerning the church's mission; I felt that it had ended. It was the era of the "Honest to God" debate. This was primarily theological and I have never been a theologian by nature, but a mystic; and mysticism, at that time to me, seemed a very insubstantial framework as a bastion against the onslaught of materialism, rationalism and the, to me, arid theologizings and tendentious quotations of Dr. John Robinson, Bishop of Woolwich.

In my unease I could only see neglected churches and closed churches and clergy going to seed. I had fallen into a furrow, mentally, and I never saw over the ridge. I had become parochial, in my first parish. I lacked the stimulus of colleagues, especially Gaston Harward. Then we had been able to laugh at the annoying oddities of a parishioner; alone I mused too much on those annoyances and they assumed far too large proportions. I suppose I was unused to responsibility, I had been a curate a little too long and in Bewdley I had been very spoilt. Gaston had kept me in touch with the larger ecclesiastical world and Joan with her literary work that shuttled between London and New York had linked me with another world; we had had always so much to talk about. I think no curate was ever more fortunate in his superiors and, in a way, I had been too fortunate.

There were though, happy times, I gathered a lot of children for the Junior Service and I had my old people to minister to. One of these was Mrs Prattley, recently widowed, once the village postmistress. She was very frail, very erect, very correct and imbued with all the rectitude and gentility an upbringing by maiden aunts in Tunbridge Wells in the reign of Queen Victoria could give. I felt of use when I visited her, or took her out. I remember helping on Helena's birthday to choose a place for the burial of her husband's ashes. We found a place, close to the old Rector and his wife, and right by a large clump of snowdrops. "Lovely", she said, "the fair maids of February". That fitted Helena well, for I always think snowdrops have an intellectual beauty; there is wonderful structural engineering in their form; as there was in Helena. She grew prettier almost weekly, but her temper did not, again as a poet said of the snowdrop she was, "deeply self-engaged".

At this time I also used to visit a farmer's wife, dying of cancer; her grandfather had been tapisier to Queen Victoria. He used to race on ahead of the entourage to Balmoral, Windsor, Osborne, to adjust the bestowal of the Queen's favourite chairs and tables, so that she walked into absolutely familiar surroundings. This mattered more the older and blinder she became. One day this very sick woman took from beneath her pillow an envelope; from it she drew a water colour. It was of the infant Princess Beatrice, drawn by the Queen, the round little head, the plumply rounded shoulders, the very compactness was utterly Victorian; it was also utterly Helena.

In June we went down to Winchester for my cousin Val-Ann's wedding. Diana was a bridesmaid; it was also her seventh birthday. Helena was very jealous of this honour: she already wished to do all that Diana did. She almost achieved her wish for another bridesmaid was a shy little American cousin of four. This poor little girl, surrounded by gaping strangers whilst the photographs were being taken, was suddenly overcome by it all, she put down her basket of flowers and ran to her mother.

This was Helena's big opportunity: she dashed forward, snatched up the flowers and took her stand by Diana, so she appeared in the photographs. However this glory palled and soon she was climbing on ledger tombs and very firmly keeping cousin Katherine from joining her on this eminence.

Poor Willeke was wondering all through the wedding what had happened to her jewellery. She had put in a box, the things she was going to wear, ear-rings, brooch and her most valuable possession, a diamond and sapphire ring. They had all disappeared from the box. Helena said she had put them somewhere safe, but could not remember where. Only on our return, two days later, did we find them: they were in the thermos flask!

A few weeks later we went with Michael and Liz Godwin to Clyro in Radnorshire for the annual service to commemorate the memory of Francis Kilvert, the superb diarist of the last century. Whilst Liz and I attended the service, Willeke, Michael, their daughter Emma, Helena and Diana went for a walk on the hill behind the church. As we came from the service, there coming up beneath the trees, were our spouses and our children, a sight that would have enraptured the romantic Kilvert, all of them had wild strawberries in their button holes, leaves, flowers and fruit, it was splendidly rustic in the eighteenth century manner. We all squashed into the hall for tea.

Afterwards William Plomer, the poet and editor of Kilvert, read the episode from the diary about the wild children Kilvert saw at Mouse Castle. I could well imagine those larking girls as Diana, Helena and Emma. William Plomer told us how much Virginia Woolf had loved that passage, which, at one go, undermines all one's pre-conceived notions of the so-called typical prim Victorian family. I had been whisked up to the high table and soon I heard from the body of the hall a piercing wail from Helena: she was bored, so I knew that we all would have to go.

She was not bored on a visit to Mr and Mrs Betteridge at East Grove Farm a little later. It was a glorious

August day and the rambling farm, my favourite at Witley, lay under a lazy sun. Mrs Betteridge took us over meadows to a spinney where we saw badgers' sets, hens, a donkey, cows. Helena's eyes grew rounder and rounder and they noted everything.

Now and then there was a sharp contraction and I had learnt that that was the moment when her brain was registering something very particularly. Those eyes missed nothing that day, not just the animals, but a rotting stable door, a gate looped with string. I saw her gaze fascinated by the water in a shallow galvanized tin bath and then even more interestedly at the pattern of a rusting hole in a sheet of "Windolite." Some of these things she was seeing for the first time and she was storing them up as though it would be the last. The best was yet to come, a tabby kitten in the kitchen called "Tiger Tim", she hugged him to her neck and walked up and down the great flag stones in blissful ecstasy, happy beyond all measure. She carried him to the ancient aunt, who saw him every hour of the day, Helena's joy was infectious and the old face lightened as she saw with innate sympathy the kitten with Helena's enchanted eyes.

Often, though, her intensity blinded her and blinded me to her and I would wonder, "Does this child love anyone with the exception of her mother?" She could be so selfish and so assertive.

However, my eyes were opened when I returned from a conference in Oxford that summer. It was arranged that Willckc should pick me up at the Rural Dean's home. We arrived back in good time and this High Anglican gentleman asked me to view the various alterations being made to his beautiful late seventeenth century Rectory, a charming house which I can only describe as tender. I saw all and admired most. Then in a manner well suited to the house he said, "Come and see the cellar." As I might have guessed, it was well stocked. "Now, choose yourself some Madeira." I hummed and hawed to shroud my ignorance and then pounced. "Excellent, just right for the day." He then opened it in the kitchen and we went into his panelled study to savour the wine. When my second glass was nearly empty I heard the car. Willeke was at the gate. We went out to her.

Helena, too, was peering through the iron bars. She saw me and a look of the intensest shyness crossed her face, then utter delight; a delight so great she was about to burst into tears. I quickly lifted her up, she clung convulsively to me, her stifled sobs subsided. Willeke had to drive home for Helena clung as closely as possible to me. This was the first great demonstration of affection that she gave me and it took me straight back to my own childhood, for the person I loved above all other, until her death, was my grandmother; our reunions after school terms had always been charged with just such emotion. That straight garden path bordered with flowers has a special place in my memories, for a new facet of love revealed itself and I knew, without doubt, that my love was reciprocated.

That autumn we took Diana and another little girl from the parish to the Albert Hall to present purses to the Queen Mother for the Church of England's Children's Society. This was our second attempt at leaving Helena and remembering the trauma of the last occasion we arranged for Miss Wheeler to come and stay in the house, so that Helena remained in familiar surroundings. This visit was typical of our ambivalent selves. In the afternoon, we were loyal enthusiastic and clerical at the Founder's Day Festival. In the evening, Diana safely asleep, we were more *avant garde,* seeing Richard Johnson and Dorothy Tutin at the Aldwych in "The Devils"; a performance, especially by Richard Johnson that I shall never forget. Next morning we were patriotic once more, cheering the Queen as she drove down the Mall to open Parliament; it was *gemutlich* seeing the Queen Mother again, in a yellow dress standing at the window of Clarence House, also waving her daughter on.

Later at Hamleys I bought Helena a Christmas present, an engine powered by a battery that gave puffs of smoke and went tonk tonk. It was a great success with both of us. In the evening we were taken to the then much talked of restaurant and club "The Establishment".

Three very amusing Americans with an immense profundity of wit entertained us. The greatest amusement came later for me, when I was with some very sophisticated acquaintance who was being condescending to the "hedge priest." I quietly said that I had been there. It always had a devastating effect.

We returned to Witley excited and refreshed and our happiness was all the greater when we found Helena so happy with her new found friend Miss Wheeler. She had once been a governess and she never lost her patience and wonderful skill with children. Willeke noted this and with some other mothers a play-group was started giving Helena her first taste of school. Its venue moved from house to house and Helena, when it was in her home, quite thought she would be the boss of the occasion. Miss Wheeler was no fool and Helena learnt to have a very healthy respect as well as affection for her.

Christmas Eve stands out clearly, for on icy roads and in fog Helena and I set out for Tenbury Wells to buy a camellia for Willeke and a present for Diana that I had seen there. Quite often she said "It is nice, just you and I." I agreed, but added, "But what about when we have a baby in February?" "Oh, that will be lovely too."

6

DIFFICULTIES

"Yearning she hath in her own natural kind."

William Wordsworth

The winter grew even colder and in the last days of December we went to dinner at Martley Rectory, a neighbouring parish, along roads thickly sheeted with ice and walled by snow which had been sculptured by the wind into smooth abstract shapes. I wondered as we went, and even more as we returned,well after midnight, what I would do if the car stalled and would not go, or if the baby suddenly made its arrival. This, though, was an anxiety we came to ignore as the cold weather persisted and Willeke, tired of being cooped indoors day after day, wearied of waiting. We had outings, come what might. One day we went to see the river Teme at Stanford and we marvelled to see a frozen river; something that neither the children nor I had ever seen. Further on in Herefordshire the snow was piled in veritable cliffs with the road a narrow fosse in between.

At last, in the early hours of February 12th, a fortnight late, Willeke went into labour. Nurse Jones was phoned, a wonderful firm, capable woman, who set to work with a brisk will. From all the novels I had read I knew that I would have to boil water, but a request for newspaper astounded me and in my sleepy innocence I said, "Will yesterday's do?" It was the nurse's loud peal of laughter that woke me up properly! There were strange whimpering feral noises and much toing and froing of footsteps overhead as I rekindled the remains of the fire. Suddenly, over the imposed calm, Nurse Jones called imperiously, "Phone Dr. Paul and tell him to be quick." Seeing the alarm this message gave me she smiled over the banisters and said, "Everything's quite alright."

Dr. Paul arrived and the dog jumped up at him as he emerged from the snowy darkness. His wet shoes slid on the tiled floor and he fell his full length and his beautiful copper box of instruments went arching into the air. "You damned dog", he muttered justly as he ran up the stairs three at a time. As he reached the landing a new wail came pealing from the bedroom. The baby was born. I stayed in the sitting room listening to the footsteps round the bed and now and then heard Willeke's voice. Evidently all was well, but what sex was the baby? I listened harder, feeling like an eavesdropper, but after all it was my baby too. At last I heard them refer almost certainly to the baby as "her". For a spasm I was sad, then I found myself pushing away my book, Arthur Calder-Marshall's "The Enthusiast", the biography of Father Ignatius the eccentric monk of the Anglican Church in the last century, and I said, "Well, if it is a little girl she cannot possibly be as silly as this Father Ignatius." When Dr. Paul said, "I am afraid it is another little girl", I felt quite cross with him for apologizing for her.

Next day I told the girls; Diana accepted another sister with a subdued defiant indifference, she had wanted a brother far more than I a son. All Helena wanted was a baby and it was there. She was as ecstatic as she had been over the kitten "Tiger Tim". She was quite desperately eager to do anything for her and it made me feel very ashamed that I had anticipated jealousy. That was no part of Helena whatsoever.

The christening of Laura Hermione was at the end of April and the baroque church with its gilt splendour took on another aspect to Helena and ever afterwards she called it the "party church". She fell in love with the font with its three kneeling angels who supported the basin on their wings and whenever she returned there, she would bend down, peer into their faces and sometimes kiss them. It set so high a standard for fonts in her mind that she always looked at them in churches and when we returned to Ribbesford for a wedding she could not wait to see the font where she had been baptized. When she saw that it was square and with meaningless decoration, the only ugly thing in a lovely church, she dismissed it instantly, "that horrid thing." When the guests returned home Helena busied herself carrying round food, she dived between people's legs with a plate of sandwiches or cakes and rose up in the midst of groups causing mild surprise. If they were talking so much that they did not see her, she tapped them on the elbow; nothing would prevent her discharging her duty as a deliverer of food.

Yet in spite of many charming traits she remained to me an enigma. I should have accepted the fact that so much of her was myself, only feminine.

That summer I was struggling with a book that I was writing and a friend lent me a cottage in the wilds of Shropshire. There every Sunday Willeke would visit me with the children. One Sunday they arrived and only Diana and the baby were happy. Willeke looked perturbed and Helena pale and not at all pretty. She had been extremely wilful and severely ticked off. In the afternoon we climbed the Roundton, a nice circular turfy mountain, nearby. As we reached the top the rain lashed down in great windy gusts, we ran down as fast as we could, leaping over boulders, yet still we were soaked to the skin. At the cottage, Diana had her best clothes to change back into, I had a jumper and a pair of spare trousers, but poor Helena had nothing. So, as her clothes dried, she wore an aertex shirt of mine and looking at her I forgot all criticisms and wrote, "she looked like an angel, a surpliced one, for the short sleeves came to her elbow, the hem skimmed the ground and all around her were clouds of steam arising from the clothes".

It was a very trying period of her growth and her unpredictable rushings back and forth in the small house made life very wearing. I grew very irritable with her, she drained me of strength, but I did not like feeling like this towards her.

In the summer we had our holiday and I had seen an advertisement in the "Church Times" saying "Would a country vicar like a family house in London for three weeks in return for looking after two elderly cats?" I wrote to these extraordinarily generous people and we were offered their home in Highgate.

It was a solid, Forsyte kind of a house, the only one in its row in Hampstead Lane still a home, all the others had offices, studios or consulting rooms in them. The rain of that summer was not confined to Shropshire; and Helena's unexercised energy, she was now three and a half, was volcanic. At the Science Musuem she rushed madly from one working model to another, pressing buttons and only momentarily waiting to see the result. I was glad that I was not there.

I was present, though, when she caused an accident and the memory still pains me. Willeke, with Laura in a pram, Helena and I went up into the High Street to do some shopping. Willeke crossed the road to another.shop and we were commissioned to buy bread. In the baker's shop Helena panicked. I caught hold of her and explained that Mummy would soon be back. As I paid, I let go of her hand; instantly she began to charge with that particularly powerful, uncontrolled and unseeing energy of hers. She rushed to the door. I charged after her – I foresaw her beneath a bus. I called her. At the edge of the pavement her courage deserted her; she paused and then hurled herself back towards me right in the path of two old ladies. The older and frailer, white-haired and with an eye-shade on her forehead knocked into Helena, toppled and fell, her head striking the concrete slabs. Helena was frightened into stillness. I helped the old lady up and into the shop. I offered to take her home, but the offer was refused. Both she and her sister were confused. In the midst of the turmoil Helena began to charge again – I feared an even worse catastrophe. I deserted the old ladies, found Willeke, handed Helena over, returned to the ladies, but they had gone home in a taxi.

When I look at old photographs I can see so clearly how much more relaxed Helena was in her own surroundings. See her in a new situation, even one as simple as the annual Church Fete, dressed up as "Wee Willie Winkie" with a candle in her hand and you see that she is apprehensive and most insecure.

This feeling of insecurity, panic and stridency culminated in Holland in November. Willeke took the two little ones to the Hague to see her very loving but ageing parents. They were welcomed as ever, but Helena's hostility was aroused, her head stiffened on her little neck, her nose jerked upwards and her grey-blue eyes froze. She announced frequently that she did not like Dutch food, Dutch relations, or Holland itself. Alas, she did not keep these pronouncements to herself or the privacy of the bathroom, or tucking up with Mummy, but made them with all the vehemence and the publicity a child of nearly four can muster. It naturally endeared her to no one.

At the end of the ten days holiday came the news that President Kennedy had been shot in Dallas, gloom overspread the Western world and we were all forced to recognise that the mid-twentieth century was a violent time and Helena seemed a part of it.

7

A FATHER'S RESOLUTIONS

"What if earth
Be but the shadow of Heaven, and things therein
Each to other like, more than on earth is thought?"

John Milton

Oh Helena was perplexing. However, it did have its funny moments. Nearly every day Robin Pyatt, our grocer, came with his travelling shop and quite often Helena bought sweets from him. One evening he called. Willeke left her in the bath and went down to the kitchen to see Robin. "Sweets" thought Helena and the next thing I saw from the vegetable garden, where I was hoeing, was a dripping and stark naked Helena pursuing Robin up the drive calling imperatively to him. I retrieved her and Robin said, laughing, "Well, I don't expect to be chased by naked women at the Rectory."

Often I was unduly critical: I am told that fathers are very frequently with their second child. Life, though, was to give me a gentle but salutary lesson. On a dark and dreary day Helena and I set off to set seal to a long and complicated bit of business involving two families at loggerheads and I had become the arbitrator. We left the village and made towards the industrial north of Worcestershire, through that we went to Wolverhampton. From Wolverhampton we went into countryside once again, but with the unmistakable evidence of commuter-land, smart paint, very neat gardens and the, then, new symbol of arrival, a cast-iron street lamp painted white.

We found the house and both Helena and I were delighted. It was a Georgian doll of a house, a door in the middle, with three windows on either side. We were welcomed very effusively and taken round the garden. I found Helena, as I had thought she might be, a very useful brake on the venom of the woman's tongue when she spoke of her relatives. We were led into the house and were even more enchanted: it was all highly Victorian. A mass of little pictures, little chairs, flowers beneath glass domes and to really cast a spell on Helena a city of little Staffordshire china houses of every conceivable kind of architecture. A tray of tea was brought to us and Helena suddenly sensing something, snuggled up to me closely on the minute sofa, for she was afraid.

Our hostess wandered in and out pretending to look for the papers that I had been commissioned to collect. She talked loudly and compulsively. Then her two children returned from school. The daughter came in and began to play on the heavily ornament laden piano. She began to imitate her schoolmistress with, I imagine, masterly satire. This led to our being pupils and the child's innate dictatorship revealed itself. Still I had not been given the documents. Helena watched the child wide-eyed, who began to shout at us, and even to menace us, slapping the furniture, and coming closer to Helena. "Don't be so silly, sit down" I snapped. The child, appalled and surprised, sat down.

At that moment a Jaguar car drew up outside and I heard voices in the hall: a neighbour had called to take the children out to tea. I, inwardly, gave a paean of thanks to my rescuer, diluted with some pity for her. My thanksgiving was too precipitate, "I'm not going" screamed the child at her mother. A scene and a scuffle ensued and the affronted neighbour, murmuring good natured nothings, drove away.

"What can one do, Mr. Lockwood?" wailed the mother.

"I really think you should have made her go." I replied. Venom glittered in her eye and she said she would get the papers, plus an account for she had been involved in expense too. The whole situation had been explained to me and I knew that I would have to pay on my parishioners behalf fifteen pounds. When she returned with the bill I saw that it had been done hastily and my truth about the child had increased the bill by a pound. It had been worth it, though, for the horrid child had been led from our rude and un-understanding contact.

It was then that Helena and I had smiled at one another and saw only one another, for the cluttered room had lost all its beguilement. It contained only fear and tangled emotions and a terrible claustrophobia and suddenly it was revealed to me all that Anne Bronte had suffered from arrogant and unmanageable children with neurotic Mammas in rooms just such as that.

Footsteps sounded in the hall. The door opened and we were given the receipt. Amidst veiled farewells we departed. Alone in the car Helena's first words were, "What a horrid girl". And I said, "And what a horrid mother." I patted her knee and as we drove away in gathering darkness, I made a vow that never, never again would I say that Helena was unbearable. I never did.

At home we found Willeke and Diana already dressed for they were going on the school outing to the pantomime. We couldn't let them go until Helena had excitedly told them the story of our adventure and I could wave in triumph the papers that I had managed to wrest from her. As I put Helena to bed, she was all sweetness, gentleness and goodness, the episode had not been salutary to me alone.

Next day I took the papers to the old man. He turned them over in his hand, "I never thought you would get them," he said. "You've done better than my solicitor over seven years." Being a country parson is a strange task and one gets involved in matters no theological college had ever prepared one for.

Easter was very cold and left me, as it leaves most clergy, very tired and with a feeling of deflation. We had decided to go for a picnic, the day chosen was grey with a north wind blowing. Willeke said, "Never mind, we shall find a sheltered wood and the sun may well come out later." We made for Croft Castle, which none of us had seen. It was closed. We searched for woods, they all seemed very fenced and very private. However, we did come upon Bircher's Common, where a few cottages stood about haphazardly. I liked it instantly for it reminded me of Button Oak, a district I had ministered to when I had been in Bewdley. We went for a walk, the wind had turned even keener. Helena and I found a few pale primroses by a stream in a deep gully strewn with old tin cans. We were watched by an old man whose cap was secured to his head by a piece of string. Helena had now turned paler in the freezing air so we ran back to the car where Willeke poured out coffee that cooled immediately.

"We can't possibly picnic."

"Let's go home," said Diana, her invariable answer to all such problems.

"No, let's go to Hereford and have a meal out."

In Hereford it was beginning to snow and we hurried into a Chinese restaurant. Helena's eyes opened wide when she saw the lanterns with tassels shading the electric lights; we were shown to a table and given menus. Helena's interest was even greater when she viewed the waiters and recognised them as being somewhat different, I feared a loud remark on their colour. As they laid the table with knives and forks she said deeply appreciatively, "Aren't they kind." This aroused smiles from the tables by us. When the food came she was even more profuse in her thanks. The waiters loved her and smiled silently. As they brought our coffee and the bill Helena's gratitude was as glowing as her, now, warm cheeks, she grabbed the arm of the waiter and said, "Shall we help you with the washing up." The smiles around us turned to laughter and Helena did not understand.

The cathedral afterwards was, in her eyes, a fearful anti-climax. The Doll's Hospital, which we found later was as good as the restaurant and a few weeks later she returned with Willeke with some of her broken but precious family of dolls to be mended.

It was Lammas Sunday, the day in pre-Reformation times, when a loaf made from the first wheat cut that year was used in the Mass. I had made a rough corn dolly to illustrate the theme of my sermon. As I prepared the altar for Holy Communion, an elderly couple came in and sat half-way up the church. Willeke was longer than usual at her prayers for Diana was very feverish and we could not discover the cause. Helena looking about her, saw that this couple had no prayer-books, so she bustled back to the churchwarden and asked him for two. These she brought up to the strangers. As I came down from the altar, I saw them looking and listening to her. "Books", she said, "but I can't find you the place, but Mummy could." The old gentleman replied, "I think we will manage," and he gave her the sweetest smile I had ever seen in any man.

The organist arrived, the choir arrived, the congregation arrived and the pair were eyed by everyone and as I turned to go up the aisle at the end of the procession, the churchwarden nipped up and asked me if they had come to live in the village. I shook my head. At the end of the service I stood out in the sun. The strangers emerged with the congregation and the old gentleman amidst my flock said, "I wonder if we can be of mutual benefit to one another. I am the patron of a parish." As I heard these amazing words, I swiftly led him towards the tombstones for the ears there are, apparently, less curious than those of the quick. He told me his name, "Lechmere" and then I recalled having seen him at the Archaeological Society when a lecture had been given on one of his ancestors. He was Sir Ronald Lechmere of Hanley Castle. I eventually accepted the living of Hanley Castle but I know that I owe it not to my preaching, but to Helena and her delight in being a good hostess.

There was always a rapport between Helena and Lady Lechmere, even when the former was naughty. Once when lunching with her Helena just would not do as she was told about anything. Willeke picked her up and marched her out of the room and sat her on the bottom of the staircase. Helena's pride was affronted, but her defiance broke and she howled. Back in the dining room we tried to ignore the noise, but at last Lady Lechmere put down her fork and said, "I cannot bear that little one being out there, Willeke, please bring her back." Lady Lechmere is far from being a sentimental woman, she has her own very definite discipline and when Helena came back she cast a very knowing smile which Lady Lechmere, I saw, had difficulty in restraining in return. Helena was exemplary the rest of the meal.

8

DONEGAL

"The small towns of Ireland by bards are neglected,
They stand there, all lonesome, on hilltop and plain.
The Protestant glebe house by beech trees protected
Sits close to the gates of his Lordship's demesne."

John Betjeman

That weekend was one of utter disarray. Sir Ronald and Lady Lechmere had brought excitement when we were already in a state of anxiety concerning Diana with her mysterious fever. This concern was not ours alone, several children in Witley were all ill with the same complaint. To add to our problems we were due to sail to Ireland on the Wednesday, for I had undertaken a locum in County Donegal. Tuesday was the only day we could see the parish of Hanley Castle, it was also the day when my locum was arriving and the day fixed for the visit of a specialist to see Diana. Willeke and I handed the house and children over to the Rev. John Hencher and went off to Hanley Castle, only about twenty miles away. We liked all we saw and returned to Witley thinking eagerly of the possible far future, but worried about the immediate. In spite of our hurrying we missed the specialist by ten minutes, he must have thought us very casual parents. John met us with many smiles, yes, the case had been diagnosed, Measles. "It was not very difficult for him; even I knew because she came out in spots half an hour before he arrived!"

The question, now, was what to do about Ireland. I had to go, I was committed. So with our dog Shadow, as a companion, I went up to Heysham. Late on Thursday afternoon I arrived at the Irish rectory with its belt of wind torn beech trees. It seemed very large, rather forlorn and I felt very lonely.

I had not been there more than three hours when I was besieged by tinkers. It was an almost mediaeval scene, whining old women who unrolled bandages to reveal horrible sores and men with crutches. At first I was moved to pity, then horror; but as their demands became more and more rapacious I became suspicious. They alarmed me and I went round the house and the empty stabling locking and bolting everything. That night I awoke to every noise and dreamt of the I.R.A. and all the more terrifying aspects of this strange land. On Sunday, though, in the churches, I encountered Irish charm and when they discovered that I was alone I was mightily involved in Irish hospitality. I made lonely expeditions and planned where I would take Willeke and the children when they came.

At last Willeke telephoned me, Diana was very much better and I was to meet her at Belfast airport on the next Thursday. On the very minute the plane from Birmingham manifested itself, a dot in the sky. It came down and the rabbits scuttered on the runway in all directions. Diana, very pale wearing a long sleeved jumper and jeans to hide the remains of her spots was the first to emerge. She was soon followed by Helena, more round eyed than ever and with staccato bird-like movements of her head as she looked all around, Laura in reins toddling and Willeke shepherding them all. They were all wild with excitement and chattered nearly all the way to Londonderry, then Diana and Laura fell asleep, but not Helena, she never relaxed until we were six miles from Ramelton.

Next day I took them to Rathmullan to the strand. The sun was high, there was no wind, Lough Swilly gently splashed on the sand and the air was as clear as it can only be in Donegal where it is washed by rain so often. Diana recovered completely that day and the little ones went up and down and up and down to the sea for water. This was Paradise for them.

My parents-in-law came from Holland, Oma and Opa as they were called. Very sadly with their arrival Helena became crotchetty, demanding and unwell. We all knew that she was sickening for measles, but how severe, not even Diana's bad attack had warned us. She became frighteningly delirious and Willeke had to stay by her bed all day for she would wander out on to the landing and the very steep staircase.

People in Ramelton would ask me how the wee girl was and old Mr. McAvery, the verger, whom I saw so often always asked, "Have the spots come out, Yet?" "No" came the monotonous reply. "Then give her whisky, it's the only thing to turn the spots from inside to outside." I had this advice so frequently that in desperation I bought a bottle. Of course, Helena would not touch the stuff. At last they did come and she seemed to be one's traditional and quite erroneous idea of a leper.

She missed all the good weather, she was still ill when her grandparents left, so once again they failed to see that Helena did have infinite gaiety and considerable charm. Just before we returned she recovered. She looked like a wraith, but an extraordinarily lively one. There was no drooping period of recuperation; instantly she was racing across the grass and rolling down the banks beneath the beech trees.

On the last Saturday, Diana and I were determined to show Willeke, Helena and Laura the wonderful country round Donegal town, down to Killybegs and the splendid bay of Fintragh Strand. It was even lovelier than the previous week, and in Killybegs a fisherman gave us handfuls of herrings from his trawler. On the Strand we all bathed in that lovely shallow cold sea with its exhilarating waves. Then on to Glencolumcille. There we had high tea in a little pub and we were offered poached salmon. We accepted, but wondered if the poached referred not only to the cooking but the catching as well. Helena tucked into hers and looking up at her mother said, "I like salmon". It rejoiced Willeke's heart to see the little ghost eating with such a will.

On our way home we climbed up the great range of hills and then down to Ardara. We stopped there for Willeke suddenly remembered we had nothing for Sunday dinner. Whilst she sought out a butcher Diana and I went to a grocer's shop which also sold tweed and we bought a length of natural white tweed for Willeke which she made into a dress.

On Monday we tidied up the, now, so familiar

house belonging to such unfamiliar people. Doing a locum is very odd, usually you never meet the owners but one conjures up a picture of them from the odd photograph here and there; you know their tastes from their furniture; you know their intellectual interests from their books; but you know nothing of the temperament. The key to the personality is hidden maybe even disguised. At last we piled into the car to go home: the luggage on top and in the boot, together with an immense salmon we had been given; the three children in the back and Willeke and Shadow, the dog, in the front with me. We stopped for ten minutes in Letterkenny to cash a cheque, just to be on the safe side. I remember thinking how all the bank clerks looked like members of the Kennedy family. Now we were really off.

We went through the Irish Customs, then the British, through Londonderry and twenty miles beyond. The children were squabbling in the back, pushing and squirming, "Mind the poor dog." I said.

"She's not in the back with us," said Diana blithely, thinking she was in the front with us. Shadow was not in the car. Willeke, was driving, she was aghast. "What shall we do?" she asked.

"We go back".

So back to the customs we went. The British Customs were not particularly helpful but the Irish were. "No, they had not seen a dog running around."

"Wait, now," said an officer with a very intelligent face, "I've had a very busy afternoon. Go back to your car and get in, I'll be with you." We waited tensely as this alert man's brain worked through the files of his mind.

"I remember. But you, sir, were driving."

"That's right."

"There were two children in the back and one on your wife's knee. There was no dog."

"What shall we do?"

"We go back to Letterkenny."

"Terrible guilt settled firmly upon us; and Helena, realizing for the first time that Shadow was lost in a strange town, burst into tears, a loud lament, immediately chorussed by the other two. I am a most pacific man, but emergencies usually turn me military.

"Tears merely upset us and do not help the dog. Be quiet."

By the time twenty miles had been traversed Shadow was almost forgotten by the two little ones, only Diana, Willeke and I were anxious. Slowly we went down Letterkenny High Street and I went to the Police Station. I explained the situation to a very optimistic Superintendent.

"Don't worry, we'll send out a search party."

We wandered unhappily back to the bank in the Square. We saw the Superintendent marching sternly down the street, evidently he was the search party. Willeke sat disconsolate behind the wheel; suddenly her face lightened, "That old man sitting, there, outside the pub, was there when we left." I dashed across the road to him. "Have you seen a small black and white dog with a tan coloured nose?"

He rose, raising a hand in a patriarchal blessing, "Y'are alright. Y'are alright." He led me into the bar. There was Shadow, sitting on the lap of the publican's wife eating crisps. I gave the old man a drop of the hard stuff. The publican would take nothing, so I stuffed a ten-shilling note into a box labelled "The mission of the Brothers of the Novena", in a ferment of gratitude.

We were, now, so late for the boat that to delay a bit would make no difference; so we had tea there. Whilst we were having it "The search party" came to report that news had already reached him that his task was done. He had tea with us. We set off for Belfast once again, after a roll call, knowing we would be three hours late in arriving at the check point. After long delays we were allowed on board. During this time Helena, so pale, so thin, never flagged in busy interest; she never dreamt of sleeping. There was so much to see, so much to do, it was no wonder her favourite hymn was "The world looks very beautiful and full of joy to me". It summed up her whole attitude to life.

At home Miss Wheeler called. She was rapturously greeted by Helena, and they talked in the garden. Then Miss Wheeler came to the house. She looked most reproachfully at us and leapt to the defence of her darling, "What have you done to Helena?" she demanded. We explained about the measles. She accepted not only our explanation but also an invitation to come and eat salmon that evening.

9

ANOTHER NEW HOME

"Tomorrow to fresh woods, and
Pastures new."

John Milton

In November 1964 we moved to our new home in, for us, a new part of Worcestershire. The parish on its western side looks up to the long range of the Malvern Hills; on the eastern edge it is bounded by the river Severn. The church at Hanley Castle has Saxon foundations; once the castle stood within a mile of it. Of the castle nothing remains: even the remnants of the moat visible when I first came have now disappeared beneath undergrowth. The castle remains only in the name of the village, a very pretty one, typically Worcestershire, with black and white half-timbered cottages and still some thatched roofs. It is what sociologists and geographers call a nucleated village, having a manor house, where the Lechmeres live; a church; a public house and a post office. We lived in Hanley Swan which has grown up around a cross road. It has a church, built by Gilbert Scott in 1873; a Roman Catholic church built by Hansom, who also invented the cab that goes by his name and a Presbytery reputedly built by Pugin.

To the family the first delight was the Vicarage. It is a villa erected round about 1815: there are others resembling it built in the same period put up presumably when Malvern Wells was thriving as a spa and before Great Malvern came into its own in the mid-nineteenth century. The house is large, with seven bedrooms, but it is remarkably compact, there are no long corridors and no stone floors. The rooms have high ceilings and the drawing room and study have long sash windows into the garden. It has only been a vicarage about twenty years, before that it belonged to a wealthy man, so it boasts of more luxurious fittings than most clergy houses. These are a mixed blessing: three bathrooms is definitely one too many; and to have six lavatories demands, I often think, that the house needs a resident plumber more than a priest. How, though, we all rejoiced in it after the narrow confines of the open plan house and how well it comes into its own on many parochial occasions. The garden, too, is well established and boasts many trees, the best being, by the children's standards, a very tall yew with a tree hut in its branches. For more than a year we lived in it exultingly, before we ever felt that it was our own.

Helena had a room of her own, as, of course, did Diana. Laura slept in the little dressing room off our bedroom. The bootroom became a playroom, a somewhat murky place, but much, much beloved by Helena and increasingly so as the years went by.

We had only been in the house a few days when I was despondently surveying the uncarpeted and undecorated drawing room that I heard footsteps on the drive. I saw a round faced man approaching. At closer quarters I saw that under very bushy eyebrows he had round and humorous eyes. It was Dr. George Lancaster of Upton on Severn, the little town nearby. He had come to see Willeke and he asked her if she would be willing to help him in his general practice. She naturally jumped at it, so, once again, our lives were changed and a new routine and regime arose.

Over the years her work has accrued, as it does for us all the longer we remain in one place. Willeke, though, like all the Dutch, has a diluted Teuton streak, that delights in organization; and she arranged her work and the care of the children very well. They have not suffered at all – in fact they have gained – for all she earns has gone to their education. Sometimes arranging a baby-sitter has been difficult and when the little ones went to a dancing class in Upton on Friday nights, which was also Willeke's surgery night and my choir practice night, then the shuttling backwards and forwards has been a masterly piece of weaving. We were, though, tremendously helped by Mrs Lewis who came up from the village of Hanley Castle to look after the children those nights. The children were very fond of her and she of them, though, I must admit, Helena frequently played her up.

As far as the children have been concerned there has never been any tension caused by Willeke's doctoring. There, has, though, been tension with the parish, for up and down the country people are exceedingly slow to learn that a wife is not an unpaid curate. Increasingly, now, the very economic situation is forcing many clergy wives to take up jobs.

I still find it very strange the fantasies that the laity often have about clergy: they see us as a people quite apart; they see, often, our large houses and leap to the conclusion that our incomes match. I well remember, when Willeke first left Diana and me to take up the post of House Surgeon in Kidderminster and we had a housekeeper from Austria, one old lady alluded to her as "an old retainer." I recall, too, the wealthy churchwarden who found it difficult himself to find staff for his house, insisting when the Rectory was built that the kitchen window be rather high overlooking the garden, for "if you are out there you will not want a maid looking out at you." But of course, this apartness is nothing new, it is an inherited reaction to the prophet, as old as the Old Testament.

The laity want one to be different and, sometimes, I at least, must be honest and say that this apartness has enabled one to be impartial and not too closely involved in a difficult situation, such as will always arise, wherever there are people.

The life of the working mother is a hard one, it means constant planning, there is the nagging worry that someone may not have met the child, or seen the old person. These are worries men do not, usually, have to contend with. Many is the time the phone has rung and I find it is Willeke, in the middle of a surgery or a clinic, just making sure that the plans she devised have worked. For the working wife of the clergyman it is just that little more complicated : for the work of the clergyman comes right into his home. There is, however, one great benefit and the laity should be grateful for this and it is that a vicar with a working wife is far less likely to become too parochial, his wife returns to talk not of the Women's Fellowship, or the Flower Arrangers Guild, but of the world of the hospital, the school, the shop or the office, each a kingdom of its own.

So, I believe, clerical horizons are far wider than once they were. I may be accused of selfishness, or even being untrue to my vocation, but at the very outset on my ordination I vowed that I would never let myself be utterly consumed by my task. I had seen other men, twenty years ago consumed by their parishes, or some aspect of church work, they had lost all other interests. I felt them to be imperfect creatures and not an asset to the faith they proclaimed, for their world was too narrow. I had many interests in the arts and I was adamant that these should not be displaced and I had talked of it to Patrick Blakiston, my first Rector. I quoted Charles Kingsley, who had been repelled by the constant conversation of religion and parish affairs by his parents. I decried such clergy. Patrick, smiled and said, "Have mercy, David, some of those poor things have nothing else to talk about." Twenty years have gone by, the scene has changed a great deal and those, good men, faithful and true have died, but I must say that a certain dullness has departed with them. Our world is more complex, has far more problems, but it is wider.

I was not always true to my vow in those first years in Hanley; certainly I was not in Witley; and neither, the parish, nor I gained by my over conscientious anxieties. I did not spend the time with the children that I ought, when I could I often was tired, but I never, never forgot them, for my family has always been my first delight.

That first Christmas in Hanley we spent alone and as soon as the Queen's Speech was over we sped up to the Malvern Hills. The wind was cruel, whipping the little tufts of dried grass and our ears. Diana almost wept, she was "starved" with cold as we say in Worcestershire. Helena and I left everyone behind and raced to the top. Time and time again I read in my diary that Helena was the first to reach the top of a hill. It was a part of the *daimon* of her personality, she must reach a goal before anyone else. On this occasion, the top achieved, we raced back to the others who were happily munching chocolates in the warmth of the car.

Instead of driving straight home, we decided to see Colwall, on the Herefordshire side of the hill. The sun was setting in a pink sky: when we turned towards Evendine it was right behind us. There was a herd of cows in the lane and we slowly moved behind them, the farmer walking in front of us. "Look", said Helena, "how the sun shines on his ring," and truly it glinted on his signet ring on his little finger like a light in its own self.

Early in January I put Helena on the child's seat of Willeke's bicycle and pedalled down to St. Mary's School. The day had at last come for her when she could go to school, real school. It was also my day for taking assembly and it was good to see Helena so composed and so happy amongst the others. I returned happy and composed, too, for I could see she was longing for real lessons and I knew that I had entrusted Helena to two good teachers, especially Mrs Morris, who was truly dedicated to her task.

It was a year, however, in which I came to be only on the most reluctant terms with my task. I was often deeply unhappy and frequently I had been tempted to abandon my calling. That year was made still harder because Sir Ronald, who had appointed me, died rather suddenly in South Africa. He had been not only the means of my going to Hanley, but also the very cause. When he had appeared so unexpectedly in Witley, I wanted no other parish at all. His wise, gentle and humorous personality had awoken such chords in my heart I moved almost entirely to be near to him. Willeke was well aware of this; she moved because it was worth trying. Perhaps the times that I was with Sir Ronald could have been counted on the fingers of both hands, yet my relationship with him had been so true, we knew one another better than some we spend a lifetime with. His death was a bitter, bitter blow to me, redoubled when parishioners would say, "But, of course, you never really knew him," I kept silent but thought how little they knew of either him, or me to say that. I do not think he had been a Father figure to me, he had been more a living emblem of all that I respect. He would have become a prop and God has certainly removed most props from my grasp. Perhaps he intends that I walk alone; therefore I do. Yes, I do regret the shortness of my contact with Sir Ronald, for I came across him in a poem of William Plomer called the Guru.

> The father figures lie in broken pieces,
> broken eggshells
> out of which we had to break away.
> The pedestals they stood on
> serve as paving stones.
> And yet among them is the guru.
> You can recognise the guru;
> he respects you,
> he accepts you.

It was at this time I always made time to buy presents for the children. Helena loved clothes and if I was in London for a conference I always stole away during some session or other to sneak into Liberty's to buy her a dress length. I scored some considerable successes there, but the successes were not always so exalted. In the Kidderminster Woolworths I bought a yellow woollen cardigan: it had bright red, blue and green knitted flowers appliqued to it. It was adored from the start and in spite of its spangling of flowers, Helena adorned it still further with a gentian brooch of her mother. The present of all presents that Christmas was a black doll. She was exceptionally pretty, she was very strong and durable and much, much loved. Her name was Sarah.

In Helena's maternal affections she came only second to Laura, but outstripped Laura in physical cherishing. Nightly she was changed into pyjamas, every morning she was dressed in day clothes. Then another Christmas Oma sent a bridal dress for Sarah, worn on all special occasions. Her wardrobe, like Helena's, extended and every visit to Holland meant a lengthy visit to the toy department of a very large departmental store. Helena saved her pocket money for months for these occasions and there for literally hours she would pore over the suitability of this dress over that costume. Once was enough for me, for the agony of Helena's monumental decisions was matched only by the agony of my boredom.

In the summer we went back to Donegal, its charm on a second viewing was even greater. This time we took Peter Wardle, an honorary uncle, whom the girls loved dearly. One day we went along the Atlantic Drive and also visited a small souvenir shop. In the evening, when the little ones were going to bed the grand alarm was given, Sarah was missing. We searched high and low for her, we traced her last movements, she was last seen near other dolls in the souvenir shop some thirty odd miles away. I do not think any mother of a real child could have been more conscience stricken.

At six next morning she woke us ready to make the journey back. In the "pride of the morning" rain we drove back. I was not in the best of tempers, but I relented completely at the rapturous re-union in the little shed shop.

"Sarah, Sarah, I've come back to fetch you."

"You're lucky", said the shopkeeper,"Twice I could have sold her yesterday."

Again we went on that wonderful drive to Donegal, Killybegs and Glencolumcille, again we bathed at Fintragh Strand. This time though, we were nearly cut off by the tide and had to rescue our clothes from the rocks and wade through fast deepening sea. Uncle Peter took a photo of the girls there, it was very characteristic. Diana screws up her face and grins into the camera, Laura takes no notice, she is engaged in what she called "little creatures" – limpets. Helena, her usual round composite self gazes out to sea and the future, dreamy and at the same time alert.

10

ARTIST TO ARTIST SPEAKS

"There's a kind of living relationship between them."

L.P.Hartley

Back in Hanley again, I, too soon, let the tide of parish perplexities sweep over me. I became depressed and unwontedly weary. On such a day, I had curled up in a chair and Helena begged me to play with her, she got out the red and gold tin containing the Memory cards. This was a present from Holland, some two hundred beautifully printed squares, all in duplicate with birds, fishes, landscapes, mosaics, animals, abstract designs, all in vivid but never garish colours. These are placed face downwards and turning them up, you have to memorize their position and try to make pairs. I did not want to play at all, but the pleadings won me over. Squatting on the floor we turned and turned the cards. Helena very intent. My self-absorption lifted as I watched her skill, and not only her skill but her predisposition to certain cards: the elegant Delacroix-like horse; the cosy owl; the church and thc fir tree; the golden mosaic. Strange, they were the ones I liked best as well. Unlike Helena's young brain mine just could not remember them as she did. Her cards grew in a pile before her, her gaiety and her expertise infected me and I wrote: "The mind is a strange thing with a miserable and a happy side that like a coin can be flipped from one side to the other."

Yet still I was perplexed by her and as I watched huge chunks of my own childhood rose to the surface like ice floes, long hidden in the depths. I realized that I too had been demanding as a child, but I had had a doting mother and grandmother, with a great deal of leisure, to meet my requirements. There were no brothers or sisters to compete or share with. I was tempted to be sorry for Helena born in a different situation and in a quite different era, but I came to see that the loss was entirely mine. I came to see that none of us really repay the love we owe to those who love us most. I noted the coldness that could suddenly reveal itself in Helena and I had to write, "just as cold as I sometimes was with my mother." As she crept into our bed in the mornings I was interested to find that I used precisely the same words to her that my mother had used to me, "You are as cuddly as a bag of golf clubs." Helena did not yield, she was all elbows and knees; not soft and supple, but she was loving by nature and in fact she needed more love than either of the other two.

At the very end of the year, Helena and I went to stay with my cousin Val-Ann, now a Hillier. As we came to Chippenham, I told Helena that this was where Francis Kilvert had been born. We thought that we would look for Hardenhuish church and vicarage. As we very dutifully went along the maze of by-pass roads we decided that, perhaps, we had better not delay. Suddenly the elegant eighteenth century church was by the road-side. We stopped, went in and we were charmed by the white and blue of its interior and its exceedingly well-kept appearance. Helena took the greatest interest in the font, but decreed that though it was nice it was not as nice as the one in the "party church". She marched up to the altar rail, turned round and said imperiously and appropriately, "We had better say a prayer for Mr Kilvert."

In the New Year of 1966 we had a very bountiful present from Tante Didi, a wealthy aunt of Willeke's who lived in New York. It was the sum of £50 and I pounced upon it and declared very imperatively that it was not going to pay school bills, neither the coal bill, nor the oil bill for the central heating. Willeke demurred, but so faintly, I knew it was only a token of her Dutch puritanism.

On my wanderings in the parish I had met a Danish artist, also called Didi, like the aunt. She and her husband had recently returned from Kenya and she specialized in pastel drawings of children's portraits. She was much more than adept, she had genius and, as is so important in a portrait artist, had an almost uncanny ability to assess her sitters' characters. Helena was not in a good period, she was sometimes hostile and marmoreal of countenance, things were not going too well at school. Didi Gordon took some photographs of all three children. Before she took them I knew that Helena's would be a failure. She showed them to me, "Look at these," she said "you would hardly believe it was Helena." She tossed them contemptuously into the fire. One sitting and she had, in every sense, captured Helena. She drew her in half profile with a tilt to her head and in the curve of her mouth there is all her temperament, mischief with a hint of sadness. Helena who had been so difficult to photograph had been easy to draw. There were more sittings, but basically nothing was needed to improve the first impression.

With Laura, Didi had much more trouble. She was, as she said, too young to be drawn. She sat very well on Willeke's knee and Didi would say, "Look out of the window, Laura."

"I am" quite often came a rather cross reply.

Ultimately she drew a fine picture and in the process came to know not her sitter but Willeke very well. She told me things of Willeke's character that very few English women have ever fathomed and which I knew to be so true.

Diana proved the toughest of all to draw, she was eleven and at a self conscious stage. To her intense annoyance she had to go back again and again before Didi was satisfied. In the end she created a wonderful likeness and a very good picture. But Helena's is undoubtedly the best and still it leaves us for trips to London to be included in exhibitions from time to time.

"Why was Helena the easiest to draw?" I asked.

"Ah, my dear David, that is easy to answer. Helena is pure woman and so she enjoyed having her portrait drawn. She is also an artist, therefore we had so much in common, all was understood between us."

I was delighted by this penetration, but disturbed

as well. It meant that Helena had something of my Achilles' heel: to those she loved – and instantly – there was complete rapprochement which evokes mutual and abiding loyalty. It is a disposition that makes deep and abiding friendships. But as much as we like instinctively, so also we dislike, and I wondered if, like me, she would long for some areas of indifference between these extremes which have according to one's faith to be tempered and regulated.

Many, many hours have I looked at that portrait, her marble quality is in the bone structure, also in the fine texture of her skin. There is a perfect balance between her forehead, her ear and her chin and it is all balanced in absolute harmony on the column of her neck. The marmoreal quality is palliated, though, by her expression, so that, although so young, there was tremendous depth of feeling there; and as I gave that plumbless depth of affection to my grandmother, so Helena gave it to her mother.

Sometimes it was easy to forget how young she was, only five and still only coming to terms with school. Very much a child in many ways, yet with an odd maturity in matters of appreciation. Just how young she was was borne upon me when, at her first half-term, we all went for the day to Bath. She had often heard us speak of it, for Willeke and I love that city. All the way there we chattered merrily, we were *en fête.* As we entered Bath Helena's head darted from left to right missing nothing. I pointed out terraced houses, fanlights and in Walcot the very high pavement with backdoors to the houses on the road level beneath. After such a little life spent mostly in the country she looked up with amazement at the houses on Camden Crescent which rose like a cliff above us. She was fascinated but also, I knew disappointed, then came the very revealing question, "This is Bath, isn't it?"

"Yes, dear."

"But where is all the water swishing about?"

We went to the Assembly Rooms to see the Costume Museum for we knew that she would love the clothes. She went round with Laura's hand in her own at an incredibly rapid pace. I branded her as superficial only to be reproved as I listened to her observations at lunch time. She had assessed all that was of importance to her.

The Roman baths she loved, but was very reluctant to enter the chamber where the hot spring emerges; she hated enclosed spaces and this one was dark and filled with steam to boot.

In March Willeke took Helena to see Mr Sinclair, the eye specialist. He is a man of great skill, knowledge and great neatness. His carefully brushed hair, his well pressed clothes, his charming professional manner always remind me of a Harley Street specialist of the twenties. He remarked upon her name, "Helena Victoria, after the Princess?"

"No, just because we like it."

"I see. I knew the Princess when I was in London, a great character, most interesting. She gave marvellous musical concerts."

He said no more, he was concentrating on her left eye, which, that winter, had begun to wander. He explained that there was an exceedingly bad fault in her vision, in fact she was practically blind in that eye; it had always been so, but her mind had corrected the visual image to such an extent that the squint never revealed itself. I was appalled when Willeke told me and I learnt that she would have to wear a patch on alternate eyes in an attempt to correct it. She also warned me that Mr Sinclair had told her that when the good eye was covered the result might be frightening as she could bump into things and fall frequently. His final words had been, "However, you must persevere."

I dreaded the covering of the good eye. Yet she never fell, she never bumped, but sometimes she would hold her head at an oddly contorted angle to fix the lens where it best would function. Occasionally there were shows of temper when the adhesive patch was removed and it stuck to her eyebrow, but she was remarkably brave and very tolerant of it, even reminding us to put the thing on if we forgot.

We came to the last day of her first term. Prayers

ended I asked Mrs Morris how Helena was doing. She said such ineffectually pleasant things, I knew that she was hedging, so I said, "Does she do as she is told?"

"Oh, so you have trouble with that do you? Well we have been very firm, kind, mind you, but firm. You see she is so bossy with the other children. She bullies them into eating their dinner and leaves her own!"

Yes, indeed, that was busy-body Helena.

11

A COMPLETELY NEW BEGINNING

"Some joys are not like the pleasures of the world, fleeting and transitory, but they are ever fresh and ever young."

C.C.Sturm

When Easter was over and our Dutch psychiatrist friend and her husband, who were touring England had gone home, we packed up for our Spring holiday. A flat in Dunster had been booked, this was an area completely new to us and we were looking forward to exploring it. An Arctic wind had gripped the country and everyone and everything looked shrivelled and furtive as we travelled down to Somerset. We were all very happy, though, and we even found a place to picnic out of the blast about twenty miles south of Bristol and, then, the sun came out and we drove on in high spirits.

Our hearts lifted even higher as we turned into the little mediaeval town of Dunster and we found our flat easily. There at the gate we stood astounded, we had never seen a garden to equal it: it was a bright blazon of flowers, daffodils, tulips, wallflowers, stocks, magnolias, camellias, jasmine and currant. It was a real garden, but it resembled much more a show piece that one might see at Chelsea Flower Show. Helena and Laura skipped about excitedly as Willeke, Diana and I unpacked the car and carried the cases to the top of the house. We lit the gas-fire, we settled ourselves in, but all of us kept going to the window to look out on the garden to see if all that glory really was true. From this attic flat we overlooked the roofs of the town and the church tower with its bells was on a level with us. After tea and a game the little ones went to bed and were very quickly asleep, longing for the morrow.

During the night the clock seemed to chime in at

the very window. It became colder so we all went to bed early, hoping to be warmer there; but it became colder and colder. At a very early hour the children crept in one by one to our bed seeking warmth; we welcomed them, thinking they might bring some, and in a measure they did. A little later, someone pulled back the pink curtains: the windows were frozen and patterned with ferns on the panes and breathing hard and rubbing the window to make a spy hole so the outer world could be seen we could see that all was under the thickest pall of snow. But the snow brought no mercy from the wind; it was relentless.

After a morning indoors, Willeke, Helena and I decided to have a walk. We plodded up the steep lane, deeply wooded, where ordinarily a fast stream ran. At the summit Willeke took a photo of Helena and me and then turned back to the other two at the flat.

"Where shall we go, Helena?"

"To the sea."

So we plodded on, coming first to a tide mark of small modern bungalows, some under construction, then to the semi-detached of pre-war vintage, then to a small village, which now adjoined Minehead. There was a row of Edwardian arcaded shops and near them a signpost proclaiming, "To the sea". We trusted its instructions and set off into a grey damp and level landscape. We paddled through a limboed meadow, crossed a railway line, and went on, by an ash path skirting allotments. It was all waterbogged and desolate and in its greyness and darkness beneath that lowering sky made me think of the first world war and Wilfred Owen. Then we approached a large structure, like a factory, composed of hangars, it, also, in that light and in that wind, looked gaunt and grey. As we came nearer we saw that it was garnished with plastic decorations.

"What is it?" said Helena.

"I don't know."

It was moated as well as barbed wired. I had never seen anything like it before. Dejected ducks came in V shaped convoys quacking expectantly at us, and it was, then, that I saw the signs over the doors, "Non-Stop Dancing": it seemed to have stopped very effectively.

"Bingo Hall" and "Laughter Parade": and there was not even a distant echo of a chuckle in the air.

The penny dropped, my brain was as frozen as the air. "It's a holiday camp." I then explained what that was. On that drab day it was not inviting. Across the road and there beneath the snow was the sand. The first fifteen years of my life were spent in Scarborough and there on the North East coast I never achieved what I did by the Bristol Channel that day, I trudged in thick snow by the sea. We walked right into Minehead chatting every inch of the way and went into the first cafe we found, a very nice one.

To be in the warmth was wondrous and without thinking I ordered a pot of tea for two and hot toast. As we waited Helena examined her surroundings. When tea arrived the waitress unhesitatingly put the pot before Helena. She beamed and poured out and bent her head confidentially towards me. When the serious business with hot water jugs and sugar was done, she said, "Won't they be jealous at home?" She glowed at the grown-upness of it all. Only as we were leaving did she see some girls, much older than herself, drinking orange squash through straws and a glimmer of regret rippled across her face. I felt guilty. She would, even on a day like this, no doubt, have preferred an ice-cream. With that instant "conning" that wise parents so unscrupulously use I adeptly said, "How childish", and a look of triumphant superiority ousted any possible regret and she agreed most wholeheartedly.

We walked through the streets to Allcombe and still I do not think we stopped talking the whole way. She was fascinated by the many houses, hundreds of small ones, belonging to thrifty citizens ending their days by the sea after toiling in Birmingham, Bristol, Manchester, and London. Looking at the houses I could imagine the slightly larger homes they had left in King's Norton, Fishponds, Alderley Edge and Lewisham. Henny said, "I know what sort of people live in the houses at home, but who live here in houses so like one another?" There was the village child speaking. We began quite sensibly to guess, here was a butcher, there a baker, an electrician lived there, and an accountant at the house on the corner. In the house with the frilly curtains lived a hairdresser, and a nurse in that neat house. Then we went quite wild. Bluebeard lived in that innocent little house, and a poisoner in that upstairs flat. In that garage there was not a car, but a red and yellow striped balloon, and the owner, a burglar, went off in it every night to do his jobs at houses in the district, always gliding in just before the dawn. We became even more extravagant and silly.

This walk to and from Minehead was the most important of our lives, as far reaching as any idyllic stroll in the Spring of a courting couple. Willeke built up a continuous relationship with Helena, solid and impregnable: my relationship with her was built in the light of sudden penetrating flashes of lightning that suddenly fused us. Basically it was always loving, but it was in our natures to be fitful, not so much critical as quizzical.

I think it was as she held my hand so trustingly on the misty allotments confident, as I was not, that we were heading for the sea, that I fell in love with her, and I fell much further in love as she poured out the tea. Quite unconsciously, very significantly and very biblically, the new relationship was marked by a new name. She was Henny.

12

PONIES

"Oh wasn't it naughty of Smudges?
Oh, Mummy, I'm sick with disgust,
She threw me in front of the judges,
And my silly old collar bones bust."

John Betjeman

Every year, in June, at the foot of the Malvern Hills, The Three Counties Agricultural Show takes place. This is a great event in the calendar of our village. It lasts three days and it covers every aspect of country life. The Three Counties are Gloucester, Hereford and Worcester. Our parish is involved in many ways; some go to see the sights, some help cater at trade stands, some show cattle, or dogs, some sell programmes. We all watch the heavy volume of traffic passing along our roads to the show ground. Our local schools have a day off for it and it was on this free day that I took Helena.

At first she clung convulsively to my hand, the weather was oppressively hot, so our hands became very clammy. I had to be patient for the sight of so many people, the tents, the tractors, the noise not only bewildered her but gave rise to those particular apprehensions of hers, endowed as she was with a vivid, but as yet unharnessed, imagination. As the afternoon progressed she adjusted herself and relaxed; she saw that, after all, it was unlikely that she would be swept away by the crowds and lost for evermore. After tea in the Women's Institute tent we walked to the arena to see a display given by the Royal Military Police, both on horseback and on motorbikes.

The crowd was thick, so I squatted down, Helena sat on my shoulders and when I stood up she could see over the people quite well. She was speechless and, I knew, spellbound for, of course, I could not see her face. I, too, remember the extraordinary grace of the lances as they were raised with the impaled tent-peg on the end. All around us we heard country voices murmuring the thought that was passing through our heads as well, "Ah, but it takes two men on a bike to spike a peg, but only one man and a good horse." All the while it grew darker and darker, there was a rumble, a flash, big spots of rain, then a deluge. With Helena still on my shoulders I ran for the nearest cover, which happened, appropriately, to be the stand of Zacharias, the waterproofers. There we waited and watched as lightning played on the hills and the rain puffed in powdery little clouds through the canvas. Helena's face shone, "Isn't it all exciting. I love the horses, but I hate the motor-bikes."

So began the "Horsey" stage. She was aware of horses and ponies everywhere. Everything fed this new interest, even a trip by the school to Weston. She returned home pale with dark circles round her eyes, but enormously pleased with life. Everything had been marvellous, the sea, the sand, the fish and chips, the gorgeous cakes – but best of all had been the donkeys and ponies and the fact that she had won the race on some poor lethargic animal. Within weeks she attended a small riding school cum livery stable and soon she was equipped with a second hand Henry Hall tweed jacket, jodhpurs, a hard velvet riding cap and I unearthed my old riding crop.

Her seat was excellent, she took to it all by nature. There was always a goal before her, to canter, to gallop, to jump and for months she anticipated an "all day ride." When that day came, it was miserably cold and the route was partly on the Malverns, near the British camp, then down to Eastnor, most of it very exposed to the cutting wind. Two girls, very much older and more advanced than Henny gave up during the morning to her absolutely incredulous astonishment. They stopped for a "bit of bait" and there Henny splayed out her hand on the frozen ground, her pony nuzzling for scraps of cake came nearer and nearer and then trod heavily on her starred fingers. She never murmured – she was mortally afraid of being sent home – so with her finger throbbing she continued the rest of the afternoon. Only when she was at home and Willeke had gently peeled off her glove did she bury her head in her mother's breast and burst into tears. Willeke examined the finger, it was broken, so she strapped it up against its neighbour and it mended quite soon. Henny soon forgot her finger but she never forgot the glory of the "all day ride".

She went in for her Brownie Pony Rider's badge. She got it, not because of her knowledge, which was by no means as ominscient as she airily believed, but because of her perseverance and her enthusiasm. The tester was interested in Henny and she advised Willeke to send her to a larger riding school where she would have a more formal training. This we did and she enjoyed it tremendously.

At the same time that riding was claiming so much of her attention, music did as well. It all began very casually whilst Diana had piano lessons from Miss Gosden; for Henny wanted to know just what was going on and ere long she had ousted a reluctant musician from the keyboard. Also, at this time, she was being taught to play the recorder by Mr Broomfield, headmaster of the Junior School to which she had moved. She loved this instrument particularly.

The Miss Gosdens, what a trio, once a quartet, two pairs of twins, all musical. Their father, a Malvern organist had been a friend of Elgar and his photograph hangs over the drawing room fire at Cockshutt Farm, a small Georgian holding on Castlemorton Common. There we would go for tea and sit round the table and eat a hearty meal and hear of their various exploits. Minny talked of her goats and unfortunately the tea had always been tainted by milk from these wretched animals. Olive would tell us of the latest wedding she had attended, a constant punctuation in her life for she had taught at a preparatory school and though it is years since she retired, her boys never forget her. Then there is the doctor, a pathologist, who has held posts in Samoa, Sierra Leone and nearer to home, Cyprus. She told us the story of how she had to test the urine of a Cypriot bishop. He came to her laboratory with his specimen, for a man, however, of his rank and his sanctity it was, of course, indecorous for him to carry it. So this black robed imposing figure was followed by a small acolyte bearing a jam jar of amber liquid with as much gravity and pomp and publicity, as if it had been the bones of St Barnabas himself.

At this household Helena's interests were entirely satisfied, there was a donkey to ride, a pony and trap to ride in, geese to feed, but I felt it a clear indication of things to come, that, once, whilst we were there, and whilst the old pony was ambling dutifully up and down the orchard, Henny was nowhere to be seen. I looked in the barn, I looked in the garden, I looked in the stable where the goats lived, I wandered to the garden. There I heard an organ, no American organ, but the real thing, which took up most of the hall and made access to the staircase a matter more of negotiation than ease. I looked through the open door and there side by side on the long stool sat Dr Gosden and Henny; they were practising psalms and hymns for the following Sunday. They were quite oblivious of me, they were in a world of music where I stand passively on the fringe.

"You try, now, I'll work the pedals and stops."

Slowly, hesitantly, Helena's fingers moved on the two manuals. A mighty but melodious sound surrounded them. The doctor smiled, Helena was awe-struck at the sound she had made. I stole away, not wishing to intrude. Back with Olive Gosden I told her where Helena was and I also asked her if Henny really had any musical ability. Like a rap it came out, a rebuke for any doubt on my part, "She has a most remarkable talent for a child of her age, an exceptionally good ear. But she often lacks application." I was gratified and amused, at once. The schoolmistress in her had revealed itself.

All that year 1966 we were troubled by her eye; there was no improvement though we had persisted with the treatment, covering her eyes alternately with an adhesive plaster patch. Even now, I find it odd that she was so patient and so enduring about it all; for making her take a pill, or a tablet, was a skirmish won only by stealth or tactics. I should have understood; it was what the dentist called her apprehensions; it was the Wordsworth in us both. Our dreams are always so much more vivid than reality; we fear the unknown, for we heighten it; when encountered it is nearly always rather tame.

It was in November that Mr Sinclair decided to operate. We knew, at the outset that it would be most unlikely to improve her sight, but it would stop the eye-ball shifting and her eyes would work in alignment. We feared scenes; but as soon as she arrived in the Eye Hospital her curiosity was engaged. Here was a new terrain to be explored and understood. Willeke left her happy and talkative. In the evening we both visited her: she had sobered but was determined to be brave; and it was a most poignant moment before we left, when she immediately got out of bed and knelt by the side to say her prayers. It was as natural as it would have been at home and there was her bent fair head and the pink frilly nightie.

The operation went smoothly next day and Mr Sinclair rang Willeke up when it was over. There were to be no visitors that day. It so happened that I had to pass the hospital on my way to the Bishop's home, Hartlebury Castle, for a meeting of the Arts Committee that night. I just could not drive past, knowing that she was in darkness there, although I knew that parents were forbidden after an operation. Trusting, though, in the power of my clerical collar I entered and after the Night Sister had vetted me, I was allowed in. She was lying very still and seemed very small. "But no one came to see me today," were her first words; and keeping rigidly still she reached out her hands to me. She told me all that had happened, obviously glad it was all over and ended, "Now you are here you can say prayers with me." So, for the second time I said prayers by her bed in the ward and she responded so fervently. I crept away down the darkened ward and rushed to the meeting. It was held in the Great Saloon, which, I think, is the most satisfyingly proportioned room in Worcestershire and beautifully decorated and restored, but I never glanced at it and I never knew what the meeting was about for my thoughts were in the Eye Hospital all the while. I was in love again with that surprising enchantress my daughter.

Two days later she was up and she asked for her nurse's uniform. The remainder of her days in hospital were spent with a bandaged head with a scrap of a Red Cross cap superimposed upon it, a striped cotton dress and an apron. She commandeered screens and a portion of the ward became inalienably her own. She was enjoying herself: all her relatives wrote and her godparents visited her. Uncle Richard brought a vast bunch of grapes which she thought too beautiful to eat and it was an outrage when we suggested she should share them. However, she quickly came round and found that the role of Lady Bountiful was just as exhilarating as being a nurse.

Auntie Liz and Uncle Michael gave her an Advent angel, a cardboard cone that was so well printed it appeared to be made of blue material with broderie anglaise wings, yellow woollen hair, a red sequin mouth and green gem eyes. She kept this in her room for years.

On the last evening spent in hospital Willeke saw the force of her will-power: she was tired; she was homesick; and as her mother kissed her goodbye, she burst into tears, choked them back and said, "I mustn't cry, it is bad for my eye;" and she did not.

13

FRIENDS AND ADMIRERS

"Energy is Eternal Delight."

William Blake

Friends. Who were Helena's friends? Before anyone else there was her sister Laura, whom she adored. No entertainment, no outing, no present had to exclude Laura. Her attitude to her was rather maternal, and, like a good mother's, constant; but it did tend, again like many a mother's, to be a bit domineering at times. A dominance which she was learning to temper, though, for as Laura matured so increasingly she resented being told what to do. There was in Helena's regard for Laura a most singular purity. Before Laura was born I feared jealousy: I was wrong. I sometimes feared it later: always I was wrong.

At the annual Village Flower Show there is a section on handicrafts; both Laura and Helena entered embroidered pictures. In the family's eyes Laura's effort was very poor and Helena as she took these entries to the Village Hall gave me a conniving look concerning Laura's, as though to say, "It's not much good, but it will please Laura." She had already confided in me that she hoped for a first herself. When, late in the afternoon, the public was allowed in, all the judging done and the rosettes and cards and comments all placed, I was confronted by Helena in the crush trying to get out when everyone else was trying to get in. She was all agog with glory. "She's got her first prize, as she hoped," I thought.

"Where's Laura?", she shouted absolutely transported with delight, "she's got a first." That was the maternal, that was true altruism; for she, herself, had only got a second.

In the village Helena had few real friends. This was

partly because they were so secondary to Laura, but also partly due to being the Vicar's daughter. There is the extraordinary barrier between clergy and laity and it often affects the children of clergy more than the parents. It was also due to imperiousness, as well: she wished to rule and it was resented. Often when children had departed we tried to explain to her that she must not be so bossy: she would listen; she would try; and then she would relapse. The trouble was her way of doing things usually was the best and it annoyed her to see some scheme, some game, being ruined by tackling it some less efficient way.

At the Junior School her isolation became greater and we saw that we would have to remove her. I shall long be grateful to Mr Broomfield, her headmaster. For when I told him, he said straightway, "I am very glad. You see, she is too quick, too vital, for the others. Some of them are slow and she gets impatient. She will like the Alice Ottley; she can be a lady there." This last old-fashioned remark amused me, but he was quite right. At her new school, after her initial trepidation, she was suddenly like a bird released from a tiny cage to an aviary – she could fly, fly and fly with a flock of companions too. It was there she found her contemporary friends and the greatest of these was Sarah Schoelles.

Sarah was in many ways diametrically opposed to Helena, it was the attraction of opposites. In looks Sarah is dark with flashing eyes, thick black hair, a bold mouth, a vivid and sometimes complex personality. Helena was built on an altogether smaller fairer scale. I remember once sitting at the back of the Assembly Hall of the Alice Ottley waiting for a concert to begin. I surveyed the choir in the tiered apse and, like any parent, looked for my daughter. It was quite a shock to me, for I was so proud of her fine features: at a distance I could not distinguish Helena from the mass of "blue-serged adolescence." So I began to look for Sarah. Soon I espied the bright daring face with its strong features and by her side, as I thought would be the case, sat Helena. She looked a little prim, her back straight, her hands folded in her lap, but now that I could see her, I recognised the faint lines of satire on her lips and mischief in her eye as she surveyed all.

She did have friends in the village and amongst our friends, too, but they were older. The first, not of Hanley, but of Hales Owen, was Margaret Willetts, a tiny schoolmistress. She and her cousin were extraordinarily good to me when I was a curate. They used to feed me on cocoa and grilled sardines at a time, before I was married, when I lived in rather indifferent lodgings. Margaret has a bird-like quality, a wren perhaps. To begin with she is five foot nothing in height; her nose is a little beak; and she has sharp shrewd eyes whose lids always lower with kindness. Her mouth is slightly pursed and apparently prim; it is not in fact; it is a slight pursing of assessment. When I first knew her she was still teaching and looking after her ailing cousin.

Her house is typical of many in the Black Country: it is semi-detached, but looks as if it is the beginning of a terrace that the builder inadvertently forget to continue. The front door is never used and one enters at the back into a glazed passage. Instantly you fall upon bookcases: the living room has three doors: to the staircase, to the hall; to the kitchen; and where there are not doors or windows there are bookcases filled with the collections of lifetimes. There is the theology and the Ruskin of her father; the poetry, English criticism and modern theology of her own. The family has a long history of non-conformity and an emblem of honour is the receipt given by a bailiff when a sewing machine was seized because they refused to pay the "Church Rate", in the last century. Yet so ineluctable are the ways of the spirit that this daughter of almost grim non-conformity has become an Anglican, bringing with her a critical acumen, a penetrating understanding, such as is not so often found in Anglican pews.

When one begins to talk to Margaret one keeps within a defined area: one must not shock. But soon you find those defines have gone for her knowledge of affairs and the ways of man are deep. In her youth she studied under de Selincourt at Birmingham University and she won a first class degree. Then so young and so acutely aware of her minute stature she refused to enter a grammar school to teach but chose juniors. She went to a school in Harborne and there she remained the rest of her teaching life. Between Margaret and Helena there was a joyous understanding and when she came to stay with us Helena would sit and talk whilst Margaret sewed. Sometimes she would take her up to her room and show her Sarah her doll, her clothes, her books, the many boxes all containing things under construction, the books containing whatever she was writing. There was nothing hidden from Margaret.

One day Helena and I were in the car visiting. We found, as one finds increasingly, many doors locked and the houses empty: the owners were out in their cars. I thought of a nonagenarian, sure to be in, "Let's visit Miss Willis." The idea was hailed with a rapture that surprised me, I had not realized she was such a favourite. We drew up at Miss Willis's house, "Why are we stopping here?"

"This is where Miss Willis lives."

"Dough", the invariable cry when things went wrong, "I thought you said Miss Willetts", and a resigned but not ecstatic visitor called on the ninety year old Miss Willis.

At Blackmore Grange, two fields beyond the Roman Catholic church of the architect Hansom, lived Miss Hilda Watts. I had seen this tall distinguished lady dressed always with Edwardian allure stalking hither and thither at great speed. One day I saw her laden with parcels, bent and marching into the teeth of a gale. I stopped the car and offered a lift; thankfully she accepted and we stowed in baskets, bags and parcels. As she seated herself the plastic mackintosh enveloping the gayer fineries of coat and hat fell back. I drove off but still she prodded and counted to ascertain the whereabouts of her manifold possessions, all the while making the politest of pre-World-War-One chatter. It suddenly halted and I heard the astounding phrase: "Oh, but now, I behold who is my most gracious benefactor. It is the Vicar."

A few weeks later, as Willeke and I returned from some ploy with the children, we saw in the sunlight, resplendent in blue with a long white chiffon scarf streaming from her shoulder like a pennant, Miss Watts. She was striding in the middle of the road purposefully towards the Vicarage. I got out of the car, ran to the back door and entered the house to the sound of a Wagnerian ring of the front door bell. I feigned delighted surprise, only the surprise was false. I ushered her to the drawing room, en passant, she placed her card with a white gloved hand on the hall table; it momentarily wavered when to its consternation it found no silver salver.

"What a charming room. Give me the eighteenth century every time."

Soon I knew that she was the granddaughter of Pugin, one of the main progenitors of the Gothic Revival. I already knew that she was an ardent Roman Catholic, steeped in its traditions and most faithful in all its practices. I learnt, from her in time how much those old Roman Catholic families had felt socially ostracized because of their faith.

"It was a great thing, Mr. Lockwood, when Queen Victoria made a Catholic the Lancaster Herald. We felt accepted when we knew that a Catholic could ride so close to the sovereign at the Diamond Jubilee." She chuckled, "Charming man he was, too. He had Lancaster Herald printed on his cards, but he had it removed after many rebuffs. You would never believe it: many people thought he was a reporter from a provincial newspaper!"

When Willeke came in more suitably clad and with her hair tidy another wave of Pinero-esque chatter lapped us. Offered tea, she refused. I discovered later that it is correct on a first social visit never to accept tea. Twenty minutes, too, was the fixed length for such a visit and, 'though many topics of mutual delight had been touched upon, she rose and made her departure.

The day was very hot. The car, abandoned by Willeke, was at the door. I offered a lift and with only the faintest protestation it was accepted. So it was I who was regaled with tea in the library of Blackmore Grange. Whether that was a social solecism on my part I never bothered to find out!

"You like books I am sure, Mr Lockwood."

I do and there were all the classics of the eighteenth

century and the nineteenth, the memoirs of Creevy, Walpole, Madame d'Arblay, and a whole section on Mrs Fitzherbert.

Often she returned to Walpole: "One of the happiest days of my life was spent at Strawberry Hill. My uncle was an architect, he had business there with the clerk of works, don't you know. The lovely house was being turned into a Seminary. I was left alone in those lovely rooms, yet, you know, not alone at all. Anyone of any importance, any fame, any intellect of the eighteenth century was there. It was filled with the friends of my reading. It was vastly diverting."

"So, you've been to Dublin. Poor, poor Dublin. It is now so different. Even the nomenclature has changed. It is no longer a capital city." Wistfully she shook her head. "But, Miss Watts, it is more a capital, now, than ever before."

"How can you say that, Mr Lockwood, when it no longer has a Court? Ah, when I was a girl I saw a State Quadrille at the Castle and I danced with the Viceroy. He remembered me, too, next day at the Horse Show. I was young, then, and it meant a great deal." Dear soul, it still did for she blushed at the memory.

Both of these women, with such a gulf, apparently, between them, were Helena's friends. When on various occasions Henny sold raffle tickets for the school, or the Village Hall, she always paid long, long visits to Miss Watts. Though, of course, I did not see it, I can see her responding excitedly, well certainly amusedly, to the atmosphere, stirring her tea, smiling, listening and storing it all up in her memory. Hence one day in the village I met Miss Watts: with both hands lifted in a kind of papal salutation she declared, "Helena is a Princess"

Evermore, at Christmas, there came a truly huge box of chocolates for "The Princesses of the Vicarage." Tact and logic made her elevate the older and the younger sister, but there was no doubt in her eyes the Princess was Helena.

She had another elderly admirer, Dr Courtney, a retired G.P., who lived nearly opposite us. He was perhaps, the most cultured man I have ever known. He, too, had an array of books: Shakespeare, the Tudors, poetry and music were his passions. He adored Helena; it was one of those last and wholly innocent affairs of the heart that the old can have. Of his worship, I think, she was totally unaware. As she came home from school, it just so happened he would be leaning on his gate. Also, by the strangest coincidence, he had a sweet in his pocket. She would walk with him in his garden, see the first snowdrops, aconites, or crocus, then come home. When she left the village school and went to the Alice Ottley she used to visit him frequently and quite unprompted. He realized this and once said to me, "It's very flattering, you know, when a young girl comes to see me, an old man, and of her own volition." When he left for Plymouth to be near his son, the two even corresponded.

The man, though, that Helena most admired was Edgar Bateman. He is a gardener, a man of great erudition, very modest, often very witty, but who loves to be alone. He appears, like a migratory bird, in the garden, at the appropriate time for the appropriate job. Helena loved to help him, to chatter and to listen. He would work on whilst she skipped about; and this youngish man of "old ruralities" said, so appositely – for it exactly described her movements in the garden – "She's like a dragonfly." So true, she hovered and darted and hovered again.

Perhaps I should be jealous of Edgar for in two respects I never measured up to him. First of all my hands were not horny: that was very desirable in Henny's eyes. Secondly I do not roll cigarettes: that was a mystic skill and she watched it with open-eyed admiration.

Diverse characters, all these, but they all had one thing in common, a most uncommon discernment.

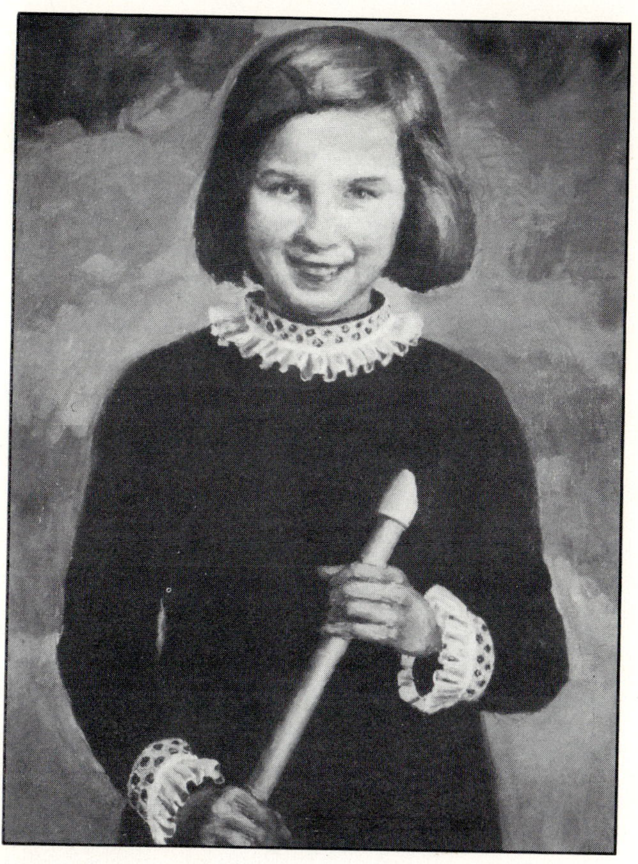

"It was the Christmas of the red velvet midi dresses."

Helena as a baby in my arms.

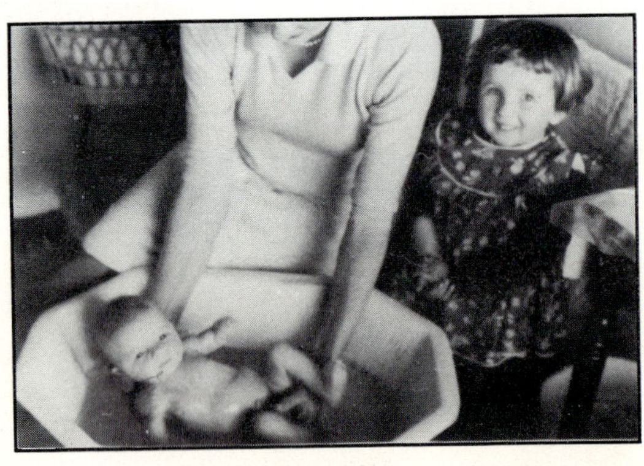

"Yes, sir, that's my baby." Helena helping bathe week-old Laura.

Willeke and Helena at Tenby.

Diana and Helena in Trafalgar Square.

Helena and I setting out for a walk in the snow at Dunster.

The Family in the garden.

14

CHERRY RIPE

"Those cherries fairly do enclose
Of orient pearls a double row,
Which when her lovely laughter shows,
They look like rose-buds filled with snow:
Yet them nor peer, nor prince can buy,
Till Cherry Ripe themselves do cry."

Thomas Campion

At the beginning of 1967 I found the children distinctly trying and my diary is full of such remarks as:-

"Children are such a nuisance."

"Helena was with us – she was a pest."

The root of the matter was that both Henny and I were unhappy. I was in one of my periodic phases of being at cross purposes to my calling; for as yet I did not know quite how much my faith meant to me. And Helena, still at the village school was frustrated. In our unhappiness we both became egocentric. There were other days as well, though. I wrote that "Helena and Laura looked very sweet in their yellow floral dresses with pique collars and cuffs. I was very proud of them".

I recall the day I wrote that for we went to see Peter Wardle and his mother at their home in the Wyre Forest, a romantic setting of a few houses built at the beginning of the century. I remember seeing them for the first time and they made me think of Tolstoy and Socialism at the turn of the century. Only much later did I discover that they were built by the St George's Society, inspired by Ruskin; and they were, indeed a part of the Art and Craft Movement and the return to Nature. All through lunch the rain fell steadily: we were all disappointed for we were determined to walk in the enchanting wood. But because we were determined an array of assorted and antique rainwear was unearthed. The two children changed into trousers and boots and over their coats and woollen caps were tied old plastic capes. In this extraordinary gear we set out walking through the trees. Laura was totally enveloped in bright blue and looked like a mobile mushroom, a very exotic one. Helena was nearly as odd, but the brown and fawn of her coverings made me think of her as one of Tolkien's hobbits.

It was the year of the Millais Exhibition at the Royal Academy and I discovered that Miss Watts wished to go. We parked the little ones with a friend for the day and went on to collect Miss Watts. Wearing flat sensible shoes she emerged but the rest of her outfit was an array of gorgeous emerald green velvet. At her direction at Paddington we boarded a No 15 bus and had "to alight at Mr Selfridge." We walked down Bond Street to Burlington House. There she wandered from picture to picture, enraptured, alert, critical and fascinatingly informed. As I saw the texture of his painting grow muddier and more academic and very often more sentimental my interest waned. But I was suddenly amused when before "Hearts are Trumps", Miss Watts said, "The mother of those girls hadn't a bean, don't you know. She spent all she had on that picture. What an investment: Each one of them was married well by the end of the season!"

Our favourites were the early clear cut, clear lined, deep shadowed and brilliantly coloured pictures of the Pre-Raphaelite period, when his youthful vigour showed itself and his aims were uncorrupted by success. As he became more famous so his sitters became more aristocratic. It was when we were looking at the picture of little girls lying in the grass beneath apple trees in bloom – one disliked, and rightly, by Ruskin – that Miss Watts said, "Now, that child's profile is Helena's exactly." It was and I looked to see if the child had been named in the catalogue. She was. It was Georgina Moncrieff, who became the famed and beautiful Countess of Dudley; whose memory I had just been in time in the 1960's to capture in Great Witley, for Witley Court had been one of her homes. I remembered being told by an old lady, a farmer's widow, how she, as a child, at the very farm where I visited, had seen Georgina ride up, side saddle of course, to see the farm and meet the tenants. "I never realized that I would never see another woman more beautiful in my life, but I did realize she was beautiful."

I thought how strange are the coincidences and contingencies of life, how sometimes time overlaps and boundaries between now and the past and another life are quite meaningless. Helena, who had lived, too, in Witley was just like the infant Georgina; but I also, prayed that my Henny, if she did become as beautiful, would never become as rich and as grand. For the great Lady Dudley had been in looks and manner, I believe, as adamantine as her jewels; and I had this fear for Helena. For though so gay, so vivacious, yet her face could suddenly be as set as stone: where did that tendency come from?

Every Sunday, that winter, we watched "Great Expectations" on the television, my favourite of all Dickens. It gripped Helena just as it had me when I was twelve and saw the film. Henny though was younger and she was so enthralled that she would forget Laura who, of course was close by her, and she would fail to put out the usually reassuring maternal hand. So Laura, frightened, would retreat behind the wing arm chair and peer round at the screen like a frightened little dog: there were quite a few terrifying episodes.

After Easter we went to Scarborough. We took a flat on Cliff Bridge Terrace almost next door to my old home. We looked out on the valley, the Spa bridge, and the sea from the same angle as I had looked at it so often as a child: it was rather strange. I showed the girls where I had played at their age and the little ones, who, just as I had, disappeared into the deep grottoes, walks and ravines of the Londesborough Gardens before breakfast. I felt just as my mother must have felt, walking round calling for those wretched children, who were upsetting entire programmes, and yet enjoying, too, the morning sun, the damp fresh air.

Whenever possible we went down to the sands and those poor celluloid windmills worked overtime. One day when they whizzed round more ferociously than usual, Willeke and I gritted our teeth and bore the cold as bravely as we could, for the children were digging equally ferociously. At last Willeke could bear it no longer: "I think I'll go back to the flat", she said tentatively.

"Yes, let's", was shouted in enthusiastic accord and three spades were flung to the ground.

When the children were in bed Willeke and I, sometimes, went for walks on the Spa, up to the Esplanade, down to the Foreshore. We went back to the Royal Hotel: alas, it had changed hands: the Laughtons had sold it and all the pictures had gone. However, the Empress was still there, still as composed, still as smoothly complexioned and still just about to move and with still a special smile for me.

We saw my mother's cousins, Sybil and Vera, and one day we went in convoy to Rievaulx Abbey via Pickering Castle and Hutton-le-Hole. Diana liked the history, Helena and Laura liked the grassy banks to roll on. By ourselves we went to Goathland and Whitby. We looked at the harbour and many little wooden shacks with oak smoke oozing out of cracks and crevices where kippers were being made. Then leaving the tired Laura with Willeke – who, too, had had enough – Diana, Henny and I climbed up the hundreds of steps to the parish church and the Abbey. To my sadness, not particularly their's, the church was locked, so they could not see that endearingly ugly and yet prettily conglomerated interior. The Abbey was open and they ran round the firm uncompromised ruins that stand so scornfully in the gales; then the girls found a stone coffin with a hollowed shape for the body and head. They took turns to fit themselves in.

On our return I found a note from Daisy Pretious, our dear but very deaf cleaner of the church, with whom one had long one-sided conversations. She informed me that she had Spring cleaned the church and not only the church, but her house; and she had something for me. When I called I found that she had repapered her room, all her pictures had gone and the large, early engraving of Millais's. "Cherry Ripe" was missing. This was produced from behind the sofa. "I want you to have this, Vicar, because it is so like our Eleanor". So home I went with it, not at all displeased; but Willeke was not quite so welcoming. Diana declared it "not exactly trendy", but Helena saw it, loved it, and begged for it. I never told her that she was supposed to resemble it, but being the woman she was, she did not need informing.

A few months later Mrs Junior gave her a lace mob cap and Henny would wear this, sitting up in bed straining to look as meek and as mild as Cherry Ripe. True the nose and mouth were alike, but there was a fire that burnt more brightly within Helena and it shone out of her eyes. This fire erupted, most often with me, then with Diana, less with her mother and hardly ever with Laura. I was regardful, sometimes fearful when I asked the question, "What will happen if she is as wilful as this when she is an adult?" I mused, but found no answer. However, an answer, at last, did come.

15

HOLLAND AGAIN

"A happy English child." *Jane Taylor*

When the summer holidays came we went to Holland where we rented the house of a school-friend of Willeke, Jane Mijnlieff. The night before we crossed we stayed with a doctor friend and his wife in Walmer. All the children were excited but Helena was more than excited when she awoke the next morning to the skirling of bagpipes, a new noise to her. The Warden of the Cinque Ports was in residence at the Castle; hence the pipes and hence the drums.

Although we left early we had to queue to board the ferry to Ostende: the sunlight poured down and reflected on the cliffs; numerous cars had stickers which we had never seen before, saying "Help Israel", for this was the time of the Israeli-Egyptian War.

The car journey on the other side seemed long: we became tired and jaded. We had promised ourselves a treat, dinner at the Korenbeurs, a handsome hotel of the seventeenth century in Goes. I wanted to take the children for a meal there where Napoleon had stayed when marching into Holland. We came to the trim little market square; we parked the car opposite the hotel and looked at the bright white damask table cloths and the shining silver candlesticks; then we looked at ourselves, grubby, travel-stained and we felt totally unable to compete with the elegance. So instead we ate croquettes with chips and drank orangeade from a self-service snack bar. Just before we left I had a look at the menu of the Korenboeurs: we could never have afforded its grandeur anyway! On we went, still a long way, and it was dark when we began to search for our temporary home in a compact little suburb of the Hague.

Willeke's mother had not been well and my father-in-law was fiercely protective of her. Living alone together they had developed, as old people do, a rhythm and a routine which they found acutely distressing to break. Knowing how badly Helena had behaved three years before, I was not exactly surprised when Willeke put down the phone and a little too casually said; "I think perhaps, just Diana, Laura and I will go to Bezuidenhout today."

The Dutch are a painfully honest people, they nearly always say precisely what they mean. Willeke is incapable of acting and though she tried, I knew that she was terribly hurt on Helena's behalf. Slowly as their defences against an encroaching world were broken, Helena was admitted and she behaved beautifully and she did not tire them with her high spirits.

However, this tiny incident threw Helena and me into one another's company more than usual. When Willeke went to see her parents Helena and I shopped: we enjoyed it so much we did it even when the others were at home. One day we asked, most politely and in, to our ears, extraordinarily good Dutch, for a loaf of bread. The reply in English was, "Sliced or whole?" – very deflating to our egos. We tried on our walks to play the game we had invented in Minehead making up fantastic careers for the owners of the houses. It was almost impossible in Holland for the Dutch have no secrets. No windows are shrouded with net, they almost brazenly sit behind their jungle of pot plants in lighted rooms proclaiming "Look, we have nothing to hide. Examine us at your will." So Henny and I did precisely that: we looked at their pictures; we looked at their books, – we seemed to reside in a very academic area; criticised their furniture; but we were disappointed, there was no romantic extravagance, no poisoners, no trainers of feline pick-pockets, no burglars in balloons.

Often we went to Scheveningen to the beach; sometimes we walked to a beach nearby. I thought as I wandered along looking at the three how William Plomer says,

"Alas for the fantasies of parents! Their children are not made in their own image." Mega Blakiston had tried to make me thank God that they are not; but more and more on that holiday I found more and more of my characteristics in Helena. The bond between us thickened and as we went off by ourselves we called ourselves "The Outsiders". It was not only the faint, oh so faint, rejection of the grandparents that had caused this, it was also the smallness of the house after the spaciousness of the Vicarage. We discovered there was a strong and demanding need in our temperaments that a portion of the day should be spent quite alone: if we lost this, then we were not happy. Therefore on the last Sunday both Henny and I refused to go to church; we had to be alone. I sat that morning writing up my diary at a fine Biedermeyer table and Henny sat reading and playing on the floor; then we had coffee together and talked. We were supremely happy.

When the others returned we went out to lunch and as the conversation became earnest between our hostess and Willeke about her parents, the little ones fidgetted – perhaps I did as well. So out we went, and they dragged me down the deserted lanes of shops in the old part of The Hague. They went from shop window to shop window and became wildly excited shouting "Kijk Pappa. Kijk Pappa." This chant became louder and louder as any serious citizen approached and as soon as they were past equally loudly they would say, "Do you think they thought we were Dutch," and peals and peals of laughter would ensue.

Two days before our holiday ended, the Mijnlieffs, owners of the house, returned. The original plan had been that we should all spend the last nights with Willeke's parents, but the grandparents' fears returned. So whilst the three elect went to Bezuidenhout, the outsiders went to stay with dear Oom Wim and Tante Suus in their cosy, cuddly, crowded antique shop of a flat. There we were cossetted outrageously; we had tea in bed; the bathwater was run for us; its temperature was taken; and we loved it all. Helena was so good she did indeed, for once, look like "Cherry Ripe" and she peered carefully at the cabinets full of Meissen, Sevres and miniatures and made a mental inventory.

We returned home in a very high wind with consequent rough seas following the Belgian and French coast most of the way, then turning sharply west and heading straight for Dover and we were battered and buffetted even more. Diana and Helena rushed to the prow of the ship; the waves soaked them and with their scarlet anoraks dripping, their faces radiant with pleasure, their spirits burning, they burst into the stuffy Saloon upon their poor mother, "Oh Mummy, it's lovely." Poor Mummy never responded for once. Unless, perhaps, to turn an even duller shade of green can be termed a reply? Seasickness had claimed its toll again.

When I was at home, before I became immersed in the affairs of the parish, I mused on my daughters. Diana is almost, not quite, I am glad to say, guileless; she is happy and a light does shine from behind her face, her spirit glows. Helena is so different, her smaller features can be stony, her smooth skin takes on the marmoreal and she will reveal nothing. Suddenly though, the flame leaps and she is a different being, alive and most vitally so. Laura's light is different yet again: it is more lambent, more loving. I should really say more apparently so.

Then it suddenly dawned upon me and I understood why I so often thought of Helena in Victorian terms. She was like my grandmother, who had been an Edwardian beauty. I sought out a photograph taken in Wakefield in the eighteen seventies: the likeness was extraordinary; the same profile; the same stoniness. I, then, remembered her telling me how she had been a very difficult child which seemed so at odds with the woman I remembered. I recalled her lovely gentle face, her supple upright carriage, her calmness and eternal optimism. The riddle of Helena was almost solved. I wrote, "I hope Helena will be as sweet, I do pray so. I pray, too, that she will have her great-grandmother's intellect as well."

I should have remarked that unlike her forbear who had been wantonly generous and always short of money, Helena was amazingly shrewd. Out shopping, or at some sale of work, she would always come away with more articles and more change than either of the other two.

That autumn Willeke made a bedroom at the top of the house for Helena. She had decided that she wanted a room of her own. She had shared one with Laura for more than a year; besides mother thought they talked far too long at night. So Willeke painted the walls; new curtains with a bedcover to match were made; "Cherry Ripe" was hung over the mantelpiece; a bookcase put up. It was a room of her own, with moreover a little dressing room leading from it. She was inordinately proud of it and when she told Dr Courtney of her domain, she included the bathroom next door, which also contained a sink and a cooker.

"I see," he said, "An establishment of your very own".

"Quite so," came the grave reply, which saw no irony.

Though the wind from the Malvern Hills whistled round this eyrie, only once, in a particularly vicious storm, do I remember her being frightened. Often she disappeared there, usually to make something she had seen on "Blue Peter" or learnt at school. As Christmas approached the whole area was entangled with secrecy. On November 5th, whilst Mummy was at Surgery, I was invited up there to see the bonfire on the village green. We switched off the light and watched the Breughel-like scene of black silhouettes against the leaping flames and the smaller fire where the roasting pig was being roasted on a spit and every now and then the place was lit by a rocket or Roman Candle in brief brilliant light, that lit us too.

Being alone added a dimension to her, she gained in confidence and with that came charm. At Christmas I took her shopping in Tewkesbury when she wore her white fur hat and muff. She held her back straight, her face had a pearly look with an excited glow beneath. As we went from shop to shop trying to find that particular present for Mummy, she drew glances from assistants and customers and whispered admiration, of which she was totally unaware, or was she? Didi Gordon had said that she was pure woman.

16

SPLENDOURS AND MISERIES

"Vain man, the vision of a moment made,
Dream of a dream and shadow of a shade."

Edward Young

Christmas was a particularly happy one; my family came to us; altogether we were twelve in the house. It was brightened greatly by Aunti Dot, a gay vivacious dark and pretty woman. She and Helena were firm friends. "Listen to that laugh" she would say. They were much in accord, both of them opened their eyes wide, both were eager for any new enterprise. Having this vast family, three generations in the house meant a lot of organizing, but one thing we had overlooked, the television. It was in one of its periodic fits of temperament, senility really, and everyone appearing on it had flattened heads. I had switched it on for a pantomime: Auntie Dot and I giggled away at all the ancient jokes and the music-hall gestures and the banal rhyming, whilst the others judged it very critically. "Let's have it off", said someone. As host, I felt bound to comply; so I was delighted when Auntie Dot said, "No, David and I love it. Just listen and laugh, you needn't look." This was so typical of her and reminded me of days when I had come home from school, when I was about twelve, and wanted to see some film or other that no one else wanted to see: Auntie Dot had always been ready to accompany me.

Christmas over, the family dispersed; but we still had parties to go to – one was at Eldersfield, the Deanery Clergy party. There Helena in a blue dress played her recorder; we played games; and the Rural Dean gave a display of magic. There was a huge tea spread out: Helena and Laura, like a pair of birds, picked and pecked together; they piled up sandwiches and cakes on their plates, and disappeared into a corner to consume it all. Then suddenly they were there again making a further choice.

When we left it was very dark; and going along the deep and narrow country lanes we could see no more than the headlamps showed; at last, on higher ground, we saw the myriad lights of Malvern strung round the hills. Immediately the children called out "The Malvern Twinkles" a sure sign of home. It was then that Helena sighed a deep, deep sigh and said with tragic pathos, "Christmas is over, thank goodness. We can now have some bread and butter and cornflakes. We've had so much nice food." We all hooted, especially as we remembered the heaped plates, but comedy can so often be so much more revealing than tragedy. I knew instantly from that funny remark that Helena, for all her curiosity, all her eagerness to experience, would temper that desire. There was the moderate in her, nothing of anything too much. I suddenly knew that the censor of her mind was well balanced and that though, like me, she would go to the pit's very brink out of sheer devilment, she would never fall in.

We were tired when we got home. Willeke put all three girls in the bath, I lit the drawing room fire. I was on my knees before it reading bits of old newspaper when the phone rang. It was Dawn, "David, something terrible has happened. Mummy is dead. She had a stroke."

"Auntie Dot?" I gasped.

I promised that I would be in Leicester with them the next day. I went up to the bathroom and told them. Willeke, whom, not an hour before Mrs Hand had said to me was looking very pretty, went haggard before my eyes. "Not Auntie Dot." That anyone so vital could be dead took a lot of believing. Helena gazed at me, then stared at the water between her knees hard and burst into tears. I ran away for her tears had drawn mine.

This 1968 was beginning ominously. Back from Leicester, I went into Worcester to collect a copy of Wilfred Owen's Letters which the County Library had bought at my request. As I came home in the snow in Willeke's little van, an approaching lorry overtook, ran into me, and I fractured my spine in four places. From being a help to my poor family I was an incubus. But that accident changed my entire attitude to life and to death. It was a mystical encounter with Eternity and I still feel that I should like to raise up a cairn of stones and anoint it with oil in the middle of Worcester Royal Infirmary, just like Jacob. For he saw a ladder with angels ascending and descending; I saw Heaven its very self. My recovery was miraculously swift and six weeks later I was home, but lying on a sofa.

When I was able to move about – fortunately, not before – there was a crisis in Holland with Willeke's parents and she had to go over for the weekend to see what was happening. On the Saturday afternoon, when Helena and I were alone, Diana was out and Laura was at a party, there was a car in the drive and out got our great friends Basil and Jean with their baby, my god-daughter. Instantly Helena became her mother; she welcomed them in; took their coats; and then sat to enjoy their company. She even sat, just like Willeke, with her hands folded and looking and smiling, just as her mother would have done, at the baby in her carry-cot. She was such a woman. However, an even greater revelation of her femininity was to come when we both went into the kitchen to make tea. Together we decided it would be easier to have it in the kitchen, so she started laying the table. "How many places?"

"Six."

Horror spread over her face; she was the hostess aghast. "Oh dear and I only bought five cakes and the shop is shut now." I just folded her in my arms and kissed her.

From being a year of accidents and death, it became a royal year. The Queen drove past our house to grace the Three Counties Show; for so many farmers of our counties had seen their herds slaughtered when the dreaded Foot and Mouth disease spread so rapidly during the winter, and the Queen came to show her concern. Never before, or since, have I seen our village so spruce, or so enthusiastic. Even I cut the grass outside my hedge, which so surprised a neighbour he asked me if I was expecting a knighthood. The day arrived for the Queen's progress, and to our garden there was a constant ferrying of all the old people where they were given coffee and cakes in the dappled shade. Helena's hostessing on this occasion was at fault; She was terrified of missing the Queen; but she was not the only one – so too were the old folk – so we moved their chairs into lines outside the hedge. Someone said to me, "I think we must tell them all to sit as the Queen goes by, then no one will fall." The sentence was barely finished when I saw distressed and indignant faces about me and one old soul voiced the feelings of them all with, "Sit in the presence of Royalty! Well, I shan't that's a fact. It isn't manners."

There was a ripple of excitement and beneath the tunnel of trees down the road appeared the car with its fluttering standard. I looked round, "Where's Helena?" At that moment she arrived: she had suddenly felt the moment merited a Union Jack and the only one in the house was screwed to Diana's bicycle, so bike and all were there. The police, as they had promised me, slowed up and the Queen came by very slowly: further up the road the crowd spilled beyond the verges and nearly brought the car to a standstill.

The Queen by, Helena, never one to waste time, strapped Diana's roller skates on and taught herself to use them in the yard. We began to ferry the old folk to their homes. It had all been so worth-while and as I helped Mrs Willis into her cottage, I felt as if I had arranged the entire proceeding from the Queen downwards for she said, "Thank you, Vicar. You did it capitally, capitally."

A fortnight later Margaret Willetts came to stay. I met her in Worcester and as we came through the flat meadowland and little orchards of Blackmore I said to her, "Would you like to meet Miss Watts?"

"If you think she would like to meet me."

I thought, a little mischievously, that a confrontation by these two daughters of Dissent, one Roman Catholic, the other Congregational, would be interesting. Besides, they had much in common in their interests, both were omnivorous readers. I pulled up at the Grange. Mac, the housekeeper, was hoeing the gravel. "You will find Miss Watts busy in the vegetable garden."

I went towards the far end of the garden and I did not see the tall vigorous form there, but as I passed the greenhouse, I did see a straw hat of truly grandiose proportions whose circumference slightly overlapped the staging for the plants on either side. Beneath this hat was Miss Watts, busy not with vegetables but with the intricacies of the plot of Orley Farm by Trollope, in a fair calfbound cover. I mentioned my mission. "Welcome, my dear David! Any friend of yours is welcome."

The tall and the stately advanced upon the diminutive and dignified and we were led to the library.

"And did you know, Miss Willetts, that the Queen has been to our parish? What a day! My taxi-man took me to the Show Ground. He asked me at what hour he should collect me. I, of course, could give no firm answer, could I? So, I said, "Half an hour after her majesty has departed. A guest must never leave before the monarch, don't you know."

Miss Willetts of Hales Owen smiled a trifle ironically.

"And when the royal standard broke over that tiny pavilion, that was my moment. I knew then, that only the wood divided my home from my sovereign's abode, albeit only a temporary one."

"So you are on your way to the Vicarage. Do you know Helena?"

"Quite well, I've known her since she was a baby."

"You are indeed privileged. That child is a Princess."

Then they talked, as I had wished them, of books, of children's books in particular: Margaret collected them. So off they chatted of Mrs Molesworth, Mrs Sherwood, Mrs Gatty – they were well away.

As we left Miss Watts gave us her personal benediction of uplifted hands over her white gate.

Margaret trotted by my side, "Well, that is a glimpse of another world. What a woman," she added admiringly.

That holiday Margaret spent even more time with

Henny, listening and talking. She heard of all her interests: riding, ponies, Brownies, school, Mrs Ward, her teacher. She played the recorder and the piano to her. Margaret was the grandmother Helena needed so badly and I see them both beneath the acacia tree, Margaret sewing. Helena talking, dancing away, but always returning to the still small intent seated figure. As Edgar had said of Henny, "She's like a dragon-fly."

In August, the National Pony Society had their annual gathering at the Three Counties Showground. Almost by accident we saw their patron, Princess Margaret, drive by. Throughout lunch, Helena talked of ponies and the show. Willeke had a clinic so could not take her. So I relented and gave up my afternoon to Helena. It was a dull day, but that could not disguise the superb beauty of the animals. The first we saw were the Palaminos and these were Henny's dream for evermore. My choice were the White Highlanders with their delicately flared nostrils; they reminded me of Landseer and Herring.

After we had seen the traps and little carriages, and examined riding crops at a stand, we walked hand in hand around the outside of a marquee where a small group was gathered. I saw the Chairman of the Malvern Urban District Council wearing his chain of office.

"Where's the Princess?" asked Helena.

Taking my cue from the chain of office I said, "She can't be far away." A small lady in a white hat with a rose in it immediately in front of us turned and bending down to Helena smiled into her face saying, "She's very close." It was, of course, Princess Margaret.

And yet, and yet, there was still so much I did not comprehend in Helena, there were caverns of swift rushing thoughts, energies, aggressions, deep underground. For the little girl, who so adored those ponies, who was longing for one of her own, when confronted by two tame deer with soft velvety horns, suddenly seized them and twisted them. Good God that made me angry.

Miss Gosden's frequent adjective at the end of a music lesson summed her up still: "Capricious. Capricious."

17

THE ALICE OTTLEY SCHOOL

"No minds were overtasked; the lessons were well distributed and made incomparably easy to the learner; there was a liberty of amusement, and a provision of exercise which kept the girls healthy; the food was abundant and good . . . her method in all these matters was easy, liberal, salutary and rational."

Charlotte Bronte "Villette"

In August we were in a farmhouse near Bideford for our holiday. There we were joined by Dawn, her husband Donald and their two girls Katherine and Jane. Katherine was some three months younger than Helena, yet slightly taller: Helena was the smallest of our girls. Jane and Laura were exactly the same age, born in the same night.

Helena and Katherine shared a great deal: a similar will to begin with: both were born leaders. So there was trouble every now and then. Willeke and I saw their differences when we went to Arlington House, a National Trust property, formerly the home of a Miss Chichester, an aunt of Sir Francis Chichester. Helena, as usual, rushed about, from room to room, show case to showcase, but at the end had seen everything and remembered a vast amount. Katherine rushed through with her, but in order to get it over.

Miss Chichester had made scrap books in order to pass those long Edwardian winter hours when nobody called. Some of these were of letter headings, ducal or coronetted, or the embossed addresses of Mayfair and the better parts of Kensington and Bayswater, an unwholesomely snobbish task. To Henny, though, the fact that a lady had lived there who did things so akin to her own avocations, absolutely enthralled her. Here, indeed, was someone after her own heart. The main bedroom was Henny's ideal, a muslin draped dressing table, a bridally veiled mirror and a writing desk. Again and again as we went round, Henny said, "She was a lucky lady."

At Westward Ho they all swam unendingly and Diana learnt to surf very successfully. On one of these days, I was making tea with the "camping gaz", a new toy, when Donald joined me at the rear of the car. As fathers will, we grumbled about the children and then Don, with all his knowledge of boardrooms and big business said, "Your Helena will end up as a very high powered executive; she can look you very firmly in the eye. She nearly quelled me yesterday with a steely look and I was in the right." How well I knew that look; I always countered it by returning it to her and lifting my nose up too. Hardly ever, though, did she use those tactics on her mother.

Henny had been in a belligerent mood when she went with the Barbers to Morwenstow. In the church of Parson Hawker, Dawn had difficulty in maintaining order. She reprimanded them and as they had marched towards the sanctuary had told them not to go past the altar rails. Helena had cast her grey eyed look and said, "I am a Vicar's daughter, I can go there" and she did.

Yes, it was high, high time that she went to the Alice Ottley School, the village was too small a world and as has happened so often in village life, its smallness had nurtured *folies de grandeur.* The Alice Ottley is an admirable institution in Worcester, the original Girls' High School, now an independent one and named after its foundress, another Vicar's daughter. She was one of those far-seeing indomitable women the Victorians were able to produce so well; wise, pious, gentle, but quite inflexible, who to this day has left her stamp upon the school. She was shrewd, she was authoritative, not without her prejudices, but on the whole they were good ones.

The school's core is Britannia House, a late seventeenth century building with fine sash windows, stone coigns and pediment, inside there is bolection panelling and a wide oak staircase. Miss Ottley joined to it a classroom, supposedly of the same style, so near it annoys me that the architect did not get the exact measurements of the old building. At the back is a large Assembly Hall, put up as a memorial for Queen Victoria's Diamond Jubilee –

this is equally Victorian, but more honest, it has a pitchpine charm of its own. At the back are the laboratories, tennis courts and the walled gardens. It is these gardens that give it a distinct collegiate atmosphere, a faint savour of St. John's Oxford.

Helena did not go there, though, but to the Junior School, Springfield, another Georgian building in Britannia Square. The ethos there comes from the old school: it is cultured, wise, unhurried and builds up a sense of responsibility in the young at its and their own pace and in their own particular way. It was a school that taught Helena to fly and to fly with others, no longer alone. With Miss Hawley, the headmistress of the Junior School, there was a clash of wills, which I rather expect she never really noticed. It was very salutary for Henny and she did not win: here was someone who could quell her and did so easily. It was, though, in her Form Mistress Mrs Newbould she found an ideal.

Mrs Newbould was modern and artistic and now more than ever, boxes, tins, cotton reels, all sorts of odds and ends were hoarded and not only hoarded but used. She tackled and finished many of the objects she saw Valerie Singleton making on Blue Peter. Henny could not have done this if she had not been so well trained by Mrs Newbould.

Her reports were good; but usually those first terms had a sting in the tail, "She must be more aware of others" and "She must learn to show her enthusiasm less noisily". Two years at Springfield taught Helena a lot and her last summer there I remember her being a Druidical attendant in a pageant to mark the Prince of Wales' Investiture year: she played her recorder with her usual delight.

I wonder if they would ever have been able to teach her mathematics? I do doubt it. Like many a peasant she could reckon her money well; she could evaluate profit and loss; but numbers as numbers had no fascination. I fear, like her father, she would find there was always some poor mug at one's elbow ready to do these repugnant tasks for one. For this same reason clocks and time meant little to her. She was very slow to learn to tell the time and even when she could she did not like doing so; anyway, there was always someone at hand to prompt one; why bother with these detested things when the world was so cram full of things of enchantment to explore. That was her philosophy. Was she also, I wonder, in some extraordinary way beyond time? Who knows?

She loved the school; I knew that she would before she even went there, because it appeals to me too. If I had been a girl it would have been the place for me. I felt that response when I first went there, years before to see the then headmistress, Miss Roden, about entering Diana. It had been true for Diana; it was even more true for Helena.

I remember being taken round the gardens by Miss Roden: as she talked with Willeke about essentials, I wandered off behind a border to the vegetable garden enclosed by old espaliered apple trees. By the sprouting broccoli there were violets in bloom, that seemed so typical of Worcestershire; but that walk also reminded me of *L'allee defendue* in Charlotte Bronte's *Villette.* I muttered something, rather incoherently, to this effect to Miss Roden. She looked at me kindly, but uncomprehendingly; she even overlooked this strange lapse and accepted Diana. *Villette* is not my favourite book of Charlotte Bronte's; but once read it is not forgotten; and the Pension Heger in Brussels, in spite of its formidable and unprincipled Principal with her system of spying, yet built up a place of learning. A place where sensibilities as well as intellect were sharpened: that was what I wanted for my daughters; and that the Alice Ottley gave them.

The year was not yet over. In November my mother's sister had to go to the Royal Marsden Hospital in London, we were anxious and awaiting news. One evening Val-Ann, her daughter, rang up:

"Mummy's marvellous – very bright, sitting up in bed."

"That's wonderful," I replied but knowing she had rung for more than that.

"But that's not all, David." There was another pause as Val gained control over her fears. I knew then, of course, that cancer had claimed yet another of my family – the demonic curse that slays half my kin. I felt bitterly angry, numb, reproachful and very rebellious with God. I looked without seeing through the open door into the kitchen and into the mirror on the wall beyond. I looked at a stranger, no self image interposed. I listened; I tried to pray for I love this aunt very dearly; and I thought of my cousin in her distress. With a heavy heart I returned to the fire and talked it over with Willeke. To have a wife who is also a doctor, who can put before one the various likely courses a disease can take is often useful, but even more it is a blessing. As she talked calmly, unemotionally, I recalled the face that I had seen in the mirror. It was me; it was Helena. "So that is where the stoniness comes from," I thought.

18

A WIDENING WORLD

"All the earth is gay
        Land sea
Give themselves up to jollity."

William Wordsworth

When two terms at the Alice Ottley were over for Helena, we all went to the Isles of Scilly after Easter, where I did a locum on the most delightful of the islands. St Martin's. The entire family journeyed there, so Dido, our dog and Khyee, our aged Siamese cat, were included. On the way down we stopped in Cheddar Gorge for our elevenses. Helena did not like it at all, its enclosing cliffs menaced her and she was uneasy. We failed her still further by taking her into Cox's Caves: for the coloured lights did not amuse her; the stalactites did not interest her in the least; and beneath a show of boredom was very real fear. She shifted from foot to foot as the guide expatiated; only as we proceeded deeper into the narrow passages did Willeke perceive that really she was very afraid. I picked her up and carried her, that only partially alleviated her apprehensions. There were no tears, no panic, just endurance, but when we turned to leave then she ran up and up the steps unable to bear it a moment longer. Even outside she ran up the road to the car, "Let's leave this horrid place."

At lunch time we were in Wellington and seeing afar off the tall obelisk on the hill we determined to picnic there. After several false turns and some dead ends, we came upon the long beech avenue leading to the monument. We let the children and the animals out: Khyee howled lugubriously and stalked alert and tail erect along the mossy stones. We went up to the monument and there all Devon seemed laid out as a mosaic before us in that lovely Spring sunlight. Helena and

Laura ran off together; their bond was that usually assigned to identical twins – a joyful union of spirit, a fusion of temperament; it was always lovely to see.

At Tavistock we stayed with Uncle Anthony at his school. Uncle Anthony is a lodestar to children, mine were no exception to his magnetism. For Helena, it was bliss to be near him and it was an even greater bliss to be back at school again. He led us to the dormitories and there they chose their beds. We went down to the dining room where he served us the largest Cornish pasties I have ever seen. Everything was new; everything was exciting; but to add comfort to all this allure, everything was familiar. Within minutes after tea Helena had a class – Laura. She found the harmonium so she conducted an Assembly – for Laura.

Very early next morning the long suffering Anthony cooked us breakfast and saw us off on our way to the Heliport at Penzance. As we drew closer to our destination, when St Michael's Mount rose like Excalibur from the sea and early morning mist, so my heart churned with horror for myself and for Helena. I hate flying and I knew Helena would. If she felt claustrophobic in Cheddar caves, what would she feel shut up in a fragile windowed box spinning through clouds? To me every moment was an agony; at each gyration I anticipated the propellor blades falling off; I looked protectively at my offspring – they were totally untroubled.

Even I joined in their laughter when an elderly gentleman sitting behind Willeke leant forward and with some alarm asked her if the propellor was alright for it seemed to him it was making a regular and horrible scraping sound. Willeke assured him the noise was not the propellor above the shuddering ceiling, but from Khyee who objected most strongly to being basketed and still more to flying.

The Chaplain of the Isles met us, showed us Hugh Town and where we could get on the launch that would take us to St Martin's. The launch came; housewives with their bags and baskets clambered on board; we heaved and pushed our suitcases and we, too, were aboard on the last leg of our journey. On the quay of St Martin's was

Clarence Goddard, the churchwarden, with his van awaiting us; and off we went to the bungalow.

Our temporary home was on a promontory looking out between the isles of St Mary and Tresco. On calm days it was like looking out upon a lake, for the rocks and islets seemed to link into mainland all around. The garden was wilderness – patches of turf and gorse bushes, but daffodils as well. The road past, where the gate had been, sloped down to Low Town in a beautiful curve that exactly repeated the curve of the bay. We made beds; we pumped water into the tank; we took possession. Diana and Helena shared a room: looking at it one would have concluded that it was Helena's alone. She had the knack of making a room wherever it was, however furnished, entirely her own, within minutes. With the careful disposal of a few of her possessions, she stamped the seal of her personality on any room. The doll Sarah, of course presided, and these tiny possessions which came from her case were all inventoried on a list.

Two days later there was a great storm; the sea was unmistakably mighty Ocean now – no mistaking it for any lake. We were worried, for Ti Etha, as the children called her, Willeke's twin sister, was to arrive from Holland. Time and again that afternoon we went to meet the launch: it never arrived. As darkness fell, we abandoned hope of her arrival that day. There was a knock on the door and there was Ti Etha. Her entire journey had been beset with trouble and as she had been preparing to spend a night at St. Mary's someone told her of a private boat going over to St Martin's. Clarence Goddard had met the boat and brought her to us. Etha not unnaturally saw the isles as windswept, rocky, tempest torn, threatened perpetually by the perilous Atlantic. She regarded us with amazement as we calmly sat by a fire of driftwood and by the light of the Tilley lamp I read aloud the non-events of "Cranford" which I had found on the shelf and which thrilled us all.

Next day she understood our tranquility, for we awoke to clear skies, as clear as any over the Ionian Sea and in Terry's boat we set off for Tresco. Beneath the sun we peeled off anoraks and walked thankfully in the shade of the eucalyptus grove. Ti Etha was enchanted, the contrast with the previous day was unbelievable. We walked on thick mushy mats of fallen camellia blooms; it was a Gauguin world with a dash of Rousseau. Without warning, in a jungle of cactus and succulents, huge hailstones fell: we rushed for shelter. Helena, Laura and I crept into a thicket of bamboo and watched the hail strike and ricochet off mesembryanthemums; we listened to them rustle in the thin dry leaves of the bamboo above. Helena looked up, "Mummy's land in the East was full of these trees, Laura," she said. Willeke had been brought up in Indonesia, the former Dutch East Indies. How typical of Henny to casually improve the hour.

One day, Ti Etha took us out to lunch in the smartest hotel in Hugh Town. It was extremely well-run. There were very few visitors, so the waiters hovered around us, almost one to each of us. They pushed in our chairs; they bent attentively; they unfolded the children's napkins with a flourish and laid them over their knees. Helena and Laura thought it quite magnificent.

After eleven one night, we three adults sat by the fire lazily thinking it was time for bed. Ti Etha said, "What's that noise?" We discounted it. "There", she said, "I hear it again." Truly there was a furtive noise in the bungalow. I picked up the lamp; went to the door and saw the faint flash of the pink hem of a dressing gown flick round the corner to the front door. I went to the children's room, their beds were empty. I wondered where they could have gone: I crept outside, round the house and through the gorse bushes to a dilapidated shed. A light shone through a chink in the boarded up window. I peeped inside: there were Diana, Helena and Laura in their dressing gowns, anoraks on top, hot water bottles on their laps, handing round a bottle of ginger beer and taking swigs. Plates of crisps and biscuits and chocolate lay before them. Their faces shone not only in the light of the candles, but in the unwonted mischief of it all. I then saw Helena's handiwork all around, milk bottles and jam jars full of daffodils and freesias. I crept stealthily back to Willeke and her sister and we all went to look at the solemn feast. Alas, Laura saw us: we joined them. The magic had gone: it was no longer a secret, so it was no longer fun.

That holiday was idyllic and although it was still April we bathed in the icy water. We had the islands to ourselves, we were virtually the only visitors. I took the Sunday services in the little church which was licked so clean with paint and varnish that it smelt like a ship. There Laura and Helena sat closely together in their blue psychedelic anoraks, Laura looking at me and Helena was rapt. But rapt with what I would wonder?

It had been this year that Henny started to go away for weekends with school friends. The first visit of all was one long planned with Meg Williams. The two girls at first projected a simple visit lasting a fortnight! We said nothing – neither did Mrs Williams: it dwindled naturally to a week. Finally it became a long weekend at half term. Henny was to say goodbye to us as she went to school on Friday morning and not return until after school on Tuesday.

Early in the week Henny began packing: she got down a large suitcase and began arranging and re-arranging everything. She seemed to take all her clothes, so that she could be clad for every occasion and every eventuality. There were games, an awe-inspiring amount of writing materials, and books. Willeke sorted out many of these things but the residue was still massive and the case would not shut. I was called upon to close it. On the very top I found a very large bible and prayer book. I just could not help laughing and said, "Henny, my dear, you are going for a weekend, not on a missionary journey in Africa."

Next day, case firmly closed, she boarded the bus extremely happily. On Saturday we wondered how she was getting on. Sunday came and just before lunch the phone rang: it was Mrs. Williams, "I think you had better come and collect Helena. She is a very homesick little girl." In the bright winter sunshine we went to collect her. We found the farm and at the bottom of the drive, waiting for us in the snow, was a very small and disconsolate little figure. The large farm, the large family, the length of the weekend, had been altogether too much.

The zest for new things was not quenched, however. There was Sarah Schoelles to stay with; but of all the places she liked best there was the home of her godmother Liz Godwin and her daughter Emma, who was in the same class at school. Auntie Liz could do no wrong in Henny's eyes: everything about her was perfect. She loved their modern home; she liked her cooking; she admired her clothes. They shared, in fact, a similar approach to life: both were creative, wishing to achieve beauty in all they undertook. Emma is very similar, too: they would sew together, or build bridges over the stream in the garden and talk and walk. Often, too, at the Godwins, she would see her old friend, whom she had not forgotten – Miss Wheeler.

Quite soon she learnt that it was not necessary to take even as much as a third of one's belongings for a weekend. I think Diana had a lot to do with this: for it was she who had to carry the case from the bus station to school. Eventually Henny became the owner of a tarten hold-all – a much prized possession, known as "the weekend bag."

19

"ABSENCE MAKES THE HEART . . . . . . "

"For love is heaven and heaven is love."

Lord Byron

In the summer the greatest of my friends, Patrick Ridgwell, came with his wife, Maryla and his two children Caroline and Jolyon, to see us. Every friend is unique, as every person is unique; but between Patrick and myself there is a strange bond – we are so different yet so alike. As our wives talked exceedingly happily in the garden and the offspring played, we went off to walk on the Malverns. We climbed the Beacon and our bachelor days of freedom were vividly recalled by a youthful party of students, one an American. The English were boasting of the height of the hills and said, "Do you realize that you are sitting one thousand, three hundred and ninety five feet above sea level?"

The American smiled and replied, "Boy, you should see me when I stand up."

We had an attack of nostalgia for our days at college in Lampeter and rambling unencumbered through Wales.

"If only I could go away without the children," said Patrick.

"Well, you can; there's nothing to stop you" and I added that I longed to see Paris again. We had hitch-hiked there in 1951.

"Why don't we?" and this odd economist added, "I tell you what I want to do, I want to go to a monastery."

So the cleric replied, "I will arrange the monastery for you, if you will allow me a few days in Paris *en route.*"

"Agreed."

Like schoolboys suddenly given a half holiday, we bounded down the hill, into the car and home. As soon as Maryla saw us, her shrewd black eyes knew something was afoot. "What have you two been up to?"

So I replied, "It is not what we have been up to, but what we are going to get up to. We want to go to France for a few days."

Willeke had done the accounts that morning – I knew it was just possible financially for me to go – she looked at Maryla and they both nodded. In fact they were so approving it almost took away the anticipated pleasure.

Three weeks later we arrived in Paris during a railway strike from a very slow and most uncomfortable train, so grim I felt sure it had transported Jews to Auschwitz. We were very weary and on a most erratic metro reached, at last, our little hotel right by the Sorbonne.

Next day was mardi: everything was shut, but it did not matter – we wandered by the Seine and on the footbridge watched a period film being made. A little stall had been erected for the actors to pause at: it had a lot of bric-a-brac and leaning against the counter was a large framed and faded photograph of Napoleon III. I then remembered this was, of course, my Empress's capital and I thought of her as Winterhalter had painted her and as I had seen her in the Royal Hotel in Scarborough and then, quite naturally, I thought of Helena. We walked that day, through the semi-deserted Les Halles and there I saw a representative of that nineteenth century past, an old shrivelled woman, with thin hair scraped back into a tiny bun on top, long skirted, aproned and wearing felt boots. She was cutting huge bunches of thyme and as she shed forth a pungent aroma into the air, so she shed forth the past. She surely had cut bunches of thyme in just that manner when Proust was writing and when the ageing Empress stayed, as she so often did, near her old home of the Tuileries. That morning I fell in love with Paris. We climbed Montmartre. We walked down Rue Lepic and saw, for Willeke's sake, the lodging of Van Gogh. Going back to our hotel along les quais we looked at prints and books. As it began to rain I asked a woman if she had a print of L'imperatrice: she had two of them; one, paired with L'Empereur, it was the State portrait. We began to haggle; the owner of the stall arrived; he was in a hurry to go, "Let them go at half that price"; the woman was horrified, "Non, non, non." "Mais oui, oui, oui," said I. With a very Gallic shrug she accepted, "Alors, les hommes."

In Worcester I had them framed in blue and gold that picked out the discreet water colouring: I hung them in the dining room. Helena, unprompted, gazed into the Empress's face, "She really was very pretty. I like her dress. I love those standing out dresses."

We had escaped from our children, but Patrick and I talked of them a great deal: we were every bit as bad as their mothers. That evening we dined in "Le Procope", a place that Patrick had discovered, supposedly patronized at one time by Voltaire. With the Empress, Helena went in and out of my mind that evening. I did not voice all my thoughts, but I think I was rather trying. I was like Shakespeare's lover,

> Sighing like a furnace, with woeful ballad
> Made to his mistress's eyebrow.

Next evening he had found an even more fascinating place – it had no pretensions to elegance whatsoever, but the most delicious food. It was next to L'Ecole des Charpentiers, and was obviously their guild headquarters. I never mentioned Henny, quite deliberately, but I thought of her. A few tables away sat a very pretty English woman rather more than middle-aged. She was obviously talented and witty; she was also very crippled with arthritis. I think she must have been a writer. She had an escort – he was too courteous to have been her husband: he quite obviously admired her. I looked at them and I wondered who would be the cultured cavalier of Helena when I was dead and gone, for I felt sure she would find one. I hoped he would be like that distinguished man and as kind and respectful. Oh I did indeed.

We left Paris, I more reluctantly than I could have imagined possible. We went to Taizé. It is interesting – with a beauty, an atmosphere and a purpose entirely of its own – but I just could not fit in to its ethos: I was in love with Paris, the Empress and Helena. It is not so strange for all three were beautiful; all three were enigmas; and all three were essentially feminine. It had been planned that I should return before Patrick, anyway; but I left even a day earlier, so that I could see Paris again. Evening was falling as we came into the city; the opalescent sunset was mirrored in the river; the journey had seemed short for I had made friends with an old Polish woman who understood my French – I hope that when I am nearly eighty I shall have her zest for life and her quest for beauty – She, too, loved Paris, her adopted home after agonising wanderings in two wars.

Next day I was determined to see all that I had missed before: I went to Jeu de Paumes for a second time and for the first time I went to Les Invalides. There I gazed at the tomb of Napoleon. I cannot admire him – the man of power does not attract me any more than power does. It seemed remote and distant but as I turned to go I found Marshal Foch buried there and that seemed suddenly homely. My grandfather, when Mayor of Scarborough, had received him; my grandmother had entertained him. "A little whipcord of a man" was her description of him. She had found his French very rapid, but she had entirely comprehended when he kissed her hand and said, "Je me vous souviens, toujours, Madame, la plus belle des Anglaises."

Back at home the summer holidays were drawing to a close, but not before a great occasion in Helena's life: she was to be her godmother's bridesmaid. And not she alone, but Laura, too, so Henny's joy was more than redoubled. Blue silk, long before, had been brought to Willeke and a mass of white organdie flowers to sew on the sleeves. The excitement was intense. The wedding day was cold and damp, so Willeke provided them both with white woollen stoles. They looked more grave than demure and treated the whole proceedings with the utmost solemnity. I was assisting in the wedding and at the close of the service as the bride and groom went into the vestry followed by the two bridesmaids, I smiled. Helena, now relaxed, beamed back; Laura gazed back, her eyes wide open most reprovingly as though I had committed some appalling solecism in the sanctuary.

At the reception the yellow flowers in their head-dresses fell out one by one, which was not surprising, for Helena quite literally pursued an usher and most ardently. He was a handsome young fellow, gay and lively and was to be married the following month. Watching her I wondered again, what sort of lover and husband she would eventually find and faintly I felt the apprehension that I suppose any father feels.

20

LEARNING ALL THE TIME

"A careless shoe-string in whose tie
I see a wild civility,
Do more bewitch me, than when art
Is too precise in every part."

Robert Herrick

The present that eclipsed all others that Christmas was a cape. She had longed for one and in Worcester a very pretty one of blue and tan tweed had been found. It had Ulster sleeves, so that in a manner it was a cape upon a cape. It also sported epaulettes and gold buttons; the cut was dashing and Henny adored it dearly. With it she wore the white fur hat and muff which were, now, faintly grey, especially when seen against the bright white of Laura's new ones.

Helena loved clothes; she had a keen sense of fashion and, usually, she kept them very tidily. There was an exception to this rule, though – her school coat, hat and blazer, which were dropped anywhere in the house where she happened to be standing. "Oh, why can't you children hang up your clothes?" I was pleased though that though Henny liked clothes, she was utterly unself-conscious of them once they were on; she did not prink before mirrors like some small girls. In fact, about her hats she could well have been more aware, for they invariably slipped to a most rakish angle. She made mistakes, too, in the combination of her clothes, but that is something anyone artistic and not bound by convention is bound to do. She was a figure of fun when one day she wished to wear a muff and cycle to church as well!

For my uncle and Dawn's sake, we wished to make Christmas, which revived memories of Auntie Dot, as different as possible. So on Christmas Day when the services were over, we had a hurried lunch and piled into the car. The sun was shining with that particular bright but shallow light of winter, like silver gilt worn by age and use. We had the roads entirely to ourselves: it was an intriguing experience passing through one somnolent and replete village after another – all the families still eating, or sitting over the remains of the meal, or washing up. It was Willeke's intention that I should sleep in the back of the car – I am usually very, very tired after the Christmas services – but I was as excited as the children and as we approached Burford, Willeke said, "You are not supposed to be giggling and chatting but resting." We halted on an empty road at the traffic lights to cross the bridge into Burford High Street. A family gathered in the window seat of an oriel window looked down upon us with surprise as though to say, "Why on earth is a family travelling at this time of day on this of all days?"

Henny suddenly became violently excited, her words tumbled and jammed, "I,I,I, know this town – it's, it's a wool town with very old houses and Mummy, Mummy, Mummy, go slowly, much more slowly, I can show you a middle aged pole outside a shop."

"A middle aged Pole!"

"Yes, yes, for people who couldn't read. It's a sign. There, there. There it is."

It was, of course, a barber's pole. In the previous July all her class had been taken on a tour of the Cotswolds to see the wool towns and enlarge on their mediaeval history. It was a visit that had fired the imagination of Helena and all her friends.

At Oxford we came upon a few more cars, but speeding down the motorway we were alone once again and silhouetted against the sky was Windsor Castle, long and grey, and we could just see the Royal Standard lifting rather lazily. On Chelsea Embankment we came upon a few more people and one or two cars. Those on foot we tried to assess by their deportment whether they were walking a dinner down, or working up an appetite. It was Henny who said, "I say, this is Laura's first visit to London." We slowed up so that she could see more and Diana and Henny pointed out all the things known to them.

"That's where we stayed with Mummy, Laura."

"Yes," said Diana, "Sir Thomas More lived there." We were just passing Crosby Hall.

"That's where Uncle Richard was a curate," I said, as we passed Chelsea Old Church.

"And there lived a painter called Rossetti and another called Whistler and up that street lived a gruff old writer called Carlyle."

"This is Chelsea Hospital where old soldiers live."

"And where Uncle John Hillier brings all his flowers for the Show."

"Look, look, look," shrieked Henny, as she recognised the Houses of Parliament, "that's Big Ben."

"Who is that?" I asked as we slid past Boadicea, and recieved from Helena the astounding answer, "Oh she fought the Romans, she was Queen of the Iceni, but I've forgotten her name."

Over the Thames and into Kent. Then started the earnest looking for the new house of Uncle Donald and Auntie Dawn before the light completely faded.

"What if we don't find it and have no Christmas dinner?" asked Laura rather anxiously. But Uncle Donald is a most meticulous and methodical man and his detailed and written and illustrated instructions led us faultlessly and unhesitatingly to the door. Katherine and Jane were soon out to greet us, followed by their parents, but no Uncle Alan – he was ill in bed with a bad bout of flu.

Henny standing up suddenly went pale, "Mummy, I think I am going to be sick." So instead of presents, instead of a gay and good dinner, she went straight to bed for she had flu, as well. The excitement had stilled all the symptoms: our arrival had confirmed the illness. She was far too ill to worry about what she was missing and lay wanly in bed, very still, without complaint. My uncle in the next room was even more ill: it developed into pneumonia, so it was a sickly Christmas.

It had been planned that Willeke and I should return home alone and Auntie Dawn was to keep the children. She had a wonderful programme for them of a pantomime and visits to museums. In the end we just left Diana and Laura. Covering the back seat with rugs and a cushion and a couple of hot water bottles we lay

Helena down. She was still too feverish to care that she was leaving Laura and her cousins and was only thankful for the immediate comforts of softness and warmth, as all are when really ill.

The journey home was much slower: there was so much more traffic. Just as when she had been a baby. Henny did not sleep but lay quiet and still watching the shadows. Only when we came down Burford Hill did she sit up to look at the little town that meant so much to her. After that, knowing that we were nearing home ground she asked every now and again, "Are we nearly home yet?"

At last we were; and back in her own room she was soon better. It was a winter that brought a real influenza epidemic to Britain: Willeke was terribly busy, but not with any further members of the family.

21

STILL GROWING

"O, children take long to grow."

Jean Ingelow

1970 opened with a crisis in Holland and Willeke had to fly over to Holland to help her parents. But it marked a new era in Helena's development: ever after we brought her home alone and left her sisters behind with Dawn she ceased to vie with them for our affection. It was as though that act symbolized in her mind the fact that she was loved just as much as her older sister and just as much as the younger sister whom she loved herself so much. Life was much, much easier.

Whilst Willeke was away, Miss Watts died in the epidemic of influenza. This was a great shock to us for we had all grown so fond of her and she was only in her early seventies. I told Diana and Helena as we were having tea round the kitchen table. Helena immediately went marmoreal, compressed her lips, put down her bread and said, "I think God is very greedy; he takes all the nice people from us. I loved Miss Watts; I ate biscuits and listened to her words." I smiled for that was what I had so often done – quite precisely. I had listened to the style frequently and not the content. It had been an amalgam of Jane Austin and Trollope, but Edwardian in thought and philosophy. Her amazing vocabulary had more than once sent me back to my dictionary. That Christmas we had received a particularly sumptuous box of chocolates, it was covered with gold brocade. The housekeeper told me, that when she was making up her parcels she said, "Mac, give me that big one for the Princess, it may be the last I will ever give her."

As a result of the accident when I broke my back I

received compensation and suddenly I had what I have never had before – some hundreds of pounds. With it I bought a cottage in Radnorshire. It was very dilapidated – the garden and orchard were grossly neglected and overgrown – nobody had looked after it for nearly ten years. It became mine on Christmas Eve. Early in January Henny and I went down to inspect our property: I felt quite Forsytian. We had some sandwiches, Jaffa cakes and chocolate biscuits and newspapers to make a fire in the range; within five minutes the kettle sang. We sat very happily amidst the squalor imagining what it might one day become. We went into the tiny parlour and there began to strip the walls of their thick mats of layered wallpaper. Henny became absolutely engrossed and though enthusiastic, never wild, she carefully folded each strip and put it into an empty tea chest, "It will light the fire next time we come." Later as we sat by the fire having our tea I told her that the range was coming out. "That's a pity," she said, "it's far too nice to spoil. I like it." She was, of course, quite right: so it was saved and restored in the dining room where the existing range was rusted through and through.

Soon it was Laura's birthday. I had found her a china tea service with a little spray of flowers on each cup. Laura opened it in our bed: she was enraptured; it was what she had wanted for a long time. As lovely as it was to see Laura's delight, it was even more wonderful to see enchantment shine from Helena as she saw her beloved sister so deeply thrilled.

Four days later Helena was ten. It happened also to be her half-term. Four of her friends joined us for lunch, then we took them to Gloucester Swimming Pool. The main pool was closed, being given over to a display, so we all trooped into a small crowded pool where the noise echoed and re-echoed of all the shouts and splashes. After an hour we brought them home. Their energy was not sapped so they played musical statues and bumps. After tea quiet descended: they all watched absolutely rapt "The Woolpack" on the television. It was a marvellous sight to see those girls of varying talent and interests all gripped by the story and by the history; they kept recognising houses they had seen on that significant outing to the Cotswolds. Their intelligences and their imaginations were kindled and alive.

As I said Helena was changing: her aggression was, at last, channelled. This was the work of the Alice Ottley School; also of Miss Gosden. Every Wednesday Miss Gosden arrived and the lesson on the piano and the recorder lasted an hour, sometimes an hour and a half, neither wishing it to end. Helena especially loved the recorder and Miss Gosden decided that she must enter the County Competitions.

It was a damp day in March when Miss Gosden, Willeke and Helena went to Worcester; all set off with a great sense of occasion, that prick of apprehension that gave a fillip to it all. Helena was by far the youngest competing. There were many people present and when it came to Helena's turn she noticed that the piano was pitched a key too high. In agony Helena looked at Miss Gosden: she smiled, "I thought a smile would work." It did: Helena transposed her entire piece. She won excellent marks and Miss Gosden returned triumphantly pleased with her pupil.

Opa, Willeke's father, came to stay. He noticed the difference in Helena: he had noticed it the previous year, but it was more remarkable now. She charmed him, not with her looks, but with the neatness of her mind and her clear grasp of logic. "She must become a barrister," he decreed. Her powers of argument made a great impression upon him, "Have you noticed that she never loses an argument?" I had not noticed it, but I had often heard the volleys of contumely and abuse she and Diana hurled at one another up and down the backstairs.

It was nearly Easter. I had seen somewhere, I could not remember where, a chocolate owl. Helena loved owls, but search though I did, I could not find one. In the end I bought an ordinary egg in a beaker with a very modern owl glaring forth with astounded eyes printed on its side. Then, one day, in an antique shop, Henny and I found two silver-plated beakers, black and ugly, with strange wooden bases. One was inscribed Bethlehem, the other Jerusalem. When we picked these up from the oddments tray the shopkeeper was surprised, so she knocked a third off the price. As soon as we were home, we got out the Silvo and polished the accretion of years away, "Aren't they lovely?" exclaimed Henny.

When the silver shone I asked Henny to fetch me the cooking oil and with a corner of the duster we wiped the bases with the oil, "Oh Daddy, what pretty wood." As I had guessed the bases were of olive wood, made for pilgrims years ago. Together we hid them and decided to give them to Willeke for Easter.

As usual after the morning service on Good Friday the children made the Easter Garden. The boys brought in rocks and moss and plastic bags bulging with sand. The girls ran round with bunches of flowers and arranged them in paste pots. They manufactured a garden with a tomb and the figures of the Risen Christ, Mary Magdalen, Peter and John and the angels; but it always managed to be very trim, almost suburban and very English. Helena, who gloried in colour and in flowers, had not yet arrived at the art of flower arrangement. Each pot she would present would be full of either forget-me-nots, primroses, or violets, "O my dear, do mix them up a bit."

After Easter, Uncle Anthony came to stay, bringing with him two bright and lively little boys, Peter and Mark Finch, the sons of his partner. With our girls they climbed the hills; they went to Warwick Castle; they played endlessly in the garden. On their last day we went to Slimbridge Wildfowl Trust – it was a bright cold day. The friendship built up over these days between the children was intense and in the car their voices rose higher and higher. Anthony, dear peaceable Anthony, was driving: suddenly exasperated by the din, he bellowed at them all in a voice I had never heard before – very deep, very commanding. It nonplussed them all and they were utterly silent; I was astounded too. Not for nothing had he been teaching these fifteen years, I perceived.

At Slimbridge, I slipped out of the car to buy the tickets; it was much more expensive than I had reckoned and only by turning every pocket out did I find enough money to let us all in. As we went round the effervescent spirits began to boil again and Mark in an ecstasy fell into a very muddy pool. Immediately Helena was all mother. "We must get these wet clothes off." Mark howled in chilled embarrassment.

"Mark, it doesn't matter. Your under clothes are dry. We'll all go into that house there; it says 'Tropical', so it's bound to be warm."

I was, by now, perturbed: "Helena darling, I'm afraid we can't. Uncle Anthony left his wallet at home and I've spent all mine getting us in."

"Oh that doesn't matter. Here's mine." She handed over a fat purse. There was enough for us all to go in. There was enough to buy us all cups of tea and still there was some left to buy Mummy and Diana a present.

Mrs Layton's wish was coming true: Helena was never short of money.

22

SUMMERTIME

"She had all the royal makings of a queen."

William Shakespeare

One Sunday in June Willeke left for Oberammergau to see the Passion Play. We saw her off at Great Malvern Station and in the afternoon, Helena, Laura and I went to the annual service in remembrance of Francil Kilvert in Clyro, where he had been for so long curate. When we arrived the church was full and we sat in the back seat. Laura could see nothing, so I told her to stand on the seat, which she did. Henny could see little more, so I told her to follow suit, but it was far beneath her dignity to do so. After the service we all went to the village hall for tea. I was swept away to sit by the preacher, the Dean of Hereford, and his wife. They chatted very charmingly and amiably to me: all the time, though, I was aware of shrieks of mirth arising from the hubbub of noise, squeals I knew well. Then there would be a long silence and I was powerless in my prominent position, but knew quite well what was happening. I turned round once to frown, to be greeted by two superlatively happy faces who waved to me! When, at last, I escaped, I found the two girls mischievous and victorious and was hailed with the information, "Daddy, I ate eleven cakes!"

The members of the Kilvert Society were then invited to Cae Mawr, the home of Mr and Mrs Dworski. There, strung along the banks of the lawn, we listened to William Plomer read portions of the diary that were unpublished. It was here, again unbeknown to me, Helena signed the visitor's book. Typically she managed to place her name beneath that of an admiral and immediately above the guest of honour, William Plomer.

Willeke's return was marked at the station with rapturous cries and a hundred kisses. At home there were more. Then she unpacked the wooden carvings she had bought for us all. Within days we were off to the Isles of Scilly again.

We left home at 10.30 pm driving down to Bristol, where we viewed the much beloved Suspension Bridge, whose graceful form was outlined with hundreds of electric light bulbs. It looked like a diamond necklace set out on black velvet in a jewellers window. That seen, Helena went to sleep and it was Laura who squirmed and squiggled. At five in the morning we killed time by driving round St Ives: the only people we saw were some bakers loading their vans with loaves. At Penzance we went into a transport cafe and had a splendid and hearty breakfast. The crossing over to the Isles was the worst sea journey I have ever made: all of the family were ill; and I think if it had lasted ten more minutes I, too, would have succumbed. The children picked up the local nickname for the "Scillonia" and talked frequently and often amongst the most squeamish company of the "vomit vessel". Yet, incredibly, within a quarter of an hour of landing we all ate another hearty meal on the pier before transferring to the launch to St Martins.

Henny kept a diary of that holiday, writing it up each day. She felt very free, very happy and entirely secure; it was her island. The innate imperiousness revealed itself. Once in a loud and contemptuous tone she demanded "Who are these strangers in our place?" When she came upon some eleven people on our beach! She was prouder, in a much nicer way, of her pink poncho and beach bag that Willeke had made for her.

We dreaded the crossing home. There was a spring tide and the launch could not pick us up for a long time, so we kept the "vomit vessel" waiting. We dashed up the gangway and off we went. How baseless are one's fears so often. The sea was calm and sparkling in the sunlight – even Willeke enjoyed the trip and seeing the great Cornish cliffs and the chines with little villages tucked in them, like wedges driven in to keep the giant's mouth open. At Penzance we bought fish and chips and ate them sitting on a wall looking down upon St Michael's Mount. The journey to Tavistock took longer than we had reckoned and when we finally pulled up outside Anthony's school, it was past midnight.

Helena was fast asleep; I lifted her from the seat and carried her up the path, into the lighted hall and up the stairs. On the landing she fluttered her eyelashes and as in the morning was instantly awake from the deepest sleep, "Where's Uncle Anthony? Where is he? I cannot go to sleep until I have said hello to him." This, I always thought, was a double compliment first of all to Anthony's Pied Piper genius and secondly to Helena's growing good manners.

Next morning we all slept until nine and when Willeke went into the dormitory to wake the little ones, their beds were empty, their pyjamas in heaps on the floor. They were not in the house; they were not in the garden or the playground. We searched frantically for them: eventually I came upon them hand in hand in a park half a mile away, "just having a look."

Anthony took us to Plymouth. On our way we saw many Exmoor ponies, "very nice, but my favourites are Palaminos." However, in the city she bought herself a souvenir, a tapestry picture to make of a pony. It hangs in our bedroom and in some way it is very like her. In the afternoon the reunion with the Finch boys took place. Whilst we finished tea they rollicked in the garden. Helena, although the guiding spirit of all their play, had become in these intervening months so much more mature, so that she had outstripped her beloved Peter. There was a certain disappointment in this encounter for her: she was not sufficiently experienced, however, to entirely comprehend the disillusionment she had partially felt.

Leaving Anthony we headed north; outside Exeter we stopped for a picnic. Helena, quick and impetuous, leapt out and slammed the door on Laura's thumb. Willeke was angry with her; I was livid – it was the second time she had done it and I said, "Do you, never, never, think of anyone but yourself?" The injustice of that angry and unkind remark hurts still, for truly there was no one Helena considered more than Laura. Ever since her illness she had felt more secure, so she was less egocentric. She was still less yielding and still when one cuddled her she was a "bag of golf clubs", but there had been a profound development in her and it revealed itself especially in her notions of her duty as a hostess, or dare I say it, a chatelaine.

An unhappy child of a broken marriage came to stay with us in order to help the mother, who was nearing exhaustion. Helena and I were playing with this little girl in the garden and without warning the child turned vicious: she kicked me on the head and when she saw it really hurt she laughed. Then she kicked Helena in the face. I slapped the child and ticked her off soundly. Helena had reeled back, tears of shock and pain ran down her face, but not a murmur came and she never retaliated. I would say that this was one of the most remarkable examples of forbearance I have ever seen in anyone.

The other side of her sense of responsibility occurred when a learned and distinguished antiquarian called to see me. He was well-known to me, but not to Helena. Very politely but equally firmly she kept him on the doorstep until she had been assured of his credentials, then satisfied, she led him into the drawing room. There she sat him down and entertained him with polite conversation. He was very amused. "That child of yours has her head screwed on well. You must marry her to a lord: she will look after his possessions well and do the honours too."

23

A LODESTAR

"I know where I'm going."

Folk Song

The long summer holiday drew towards its close and there were frequent proclamations from Helena: "I can't wait to go to school again". She had done all she wanted to do and was ready for her mind to be harnessed again. Yet there was still one expedition for her.

Miss Watts' home had been sold up. I had missed the sale notice because of our holiday; and was told that the auction was in progress late in the afternoon. I raced round and was there for the last ten lots. I had wanted a momento of her, so when the auctioneer described a picture as an oriental scene I could see that it was a picture of the Virgin Mary, I bought it for £2. When the room was deserted I went up to look at my purchase. As I was regarding it a thought went through my head which was suddenly spoken by Colonel Robertson, my next door neighbour, who is very knowledgeable about antiques, "It looks to me remarkably like a Burne-Jones." So acting upon this hunch, on a very hot afternoon, Henny and I went with the picture to the Birmingham Art Gallery. We waited in a little cubicle where an interestingly dressed young lady joined us. She brought with her, though, an air of having seen a thousand poor daubs in this tiny room and of having had to tactfully and gently debunk all hopes. As I unwrapped the brown paper wrapping I related its provenance. She looked at it and the tact fell away and the interesting young woman became herself interested. We arranged to leave it there for the great expert on Burne-Jones who was to visit the gallery some weeks later.

Henny and I were free: we looked at china and silver; but I was really heading her for the Pre-Raphaelites – I felt that it was important for her that "every picture should tell a story". We stood before "The Last of England". She was intrigued by the baby's hand that appears from within the mother's shawl and she wanted to know why they had "those cabbages in those nets". She looked at Millais' "The Rainbow". "Nice colours" was her comment, "but it's not quite real, is it?" The picture she liked best was by Dyce, "The Woman at the well in Samaria": when she could not buy a postcard of this she was very disappointed, reverted to ponies and bought a Stubbs, which we had not seen.

She was interested; her curiosity was aroused; but I must also admit that the chocolate biscuits in the restaurant were as equally worthy of comment and admiration from her as the pictures. That did not stop me dreaming, though; and I imagined walking through many galleries in Europe with her as my companion in the future.

A week later we had the tragic death of a young man in the village; his poor young widow was plunged into a maelstrom of grief, guilt and incomprehension, such as all suicides cause. The funeral was a tremendous ordeal and, as on such occasions always occurs, the ghouls appeared to gape. The widow dressed with her habitual sense of style. When all the obsequies were over and the bakemeats eaten, she came to the Vicarage alone to express her thanks. Helena answered the doorbell, swiftly surveyed the black dress and the trailing chiffon scarf and said, "I say, you DO look nice."

The poor girl looked surprised and then happy and pleased for the first time for some weeks.

Dido, the dog, had puppies – five lovely pedigree King Charles' Cavalier Spaniels. All three children took the keenest interest in them: Diana's was biological; Helena's was maternal; Laura's was just the wonder of something small and new. The time came for them to be sold. One day we found a note pushed through our letter box saying that a General would be calling at 12 am on his return from London on Sunday.

That Sunday happened to be St Luke's Day: I had asked a doctor from Malvern to come to preach and Willeke was to read one of the lessons. The doctor chose for his theme an exposition of the whole of the book of Job. His sermon was but half-way through when I heard the church bell strike the hour. I knew that a man with such neat handwriting as the General would also be meticulously punctual: I was anxious. Willeke, however, with her usual forethought had left instructions with Helena, "Entertain the General; show him the puppies; take him round the garden; but don't let him go."

"What's the price, Mummy?"

"It is twenty guineas, but don't tell him that."

Fully twenty minutes later Willeke arrived home and there was the General being led round the garden in a cloud of laughter and chatter. Willeke came to business; the General smiled, "It's all done. I've made my choice."

"But you don't know the price."

"Oh yes, Helena and I have agreed on twenty guineas."

School was romping by and it was one long enchantment. Day after day the front door would open and a gay high voice would call "Hello" and when asked what sort of a day it had been, almost invariably the answer was, "Oh a lovely one." She had her friends, especially Sarah; she also had a very perceptive form mistress, Miss Phillips. She noted the marmoreal look and the penetrating eye; she also noticed that of all things what Helena needed most was love. She saw how Helena came into the form room, went straight to her desk, sharpened her pencils, arranged her books and, when all that was done, talked to her friends. She recognised immediately that here was a child to be won and that if she did not win her affection, then the relationship would be irrevocably lost. She won it. Later she said, "But, you know, she was sometimes like a high powered executive and if I was slow, or muddled taking the roll call, I could feel her eyes glaring at me, as if to say, "get on with it, you silly old fool: we've work to do."

That Miss Phillips was a musician helped immensely and this made another bridge between them. Henny's boisterousness was channelled still more; her horizons were widening and there was always Diana to catch up with and, if possible, overtake. So when, "O" levels looming, Diana got out her homework on the kitchen table by the Aga, so too did Helena. Soon Laura joined them and they had to give her simple sums, spellings and tables to keep her quiet.

Nearing Christmas, the Roman Catholic Benedictine Nuns of Stanbrook Abbey decided to have an oecumenical Carol Service. At a committee meeting, Dame Felicitas sighed and said, "What we need is a recorder here." They were so deep in music talking of ritornellos and the like, of which I was woefully ignorant, so I was not really listening; but this I did understand and I offered Helena. They immediately gave me the music she had to play. Goodness, we were busy then, as we were having a Nativity play in our church as well; and in this Helena had two parts, a shepherd boy when she played her recorder, and later with a beard she was one of the Magi. The Sunday before Christmas came: there was a full scale rehearsal in the morning with the added ravishment of the attendance of a photographer from the local press. By evening Helena's tension was at it's fullest stretch. The church was full; the play began; the boys spoke up well; all was going like clockwork until one shepherd said to Helena, "Play us a tune, lad."

"Alright then." She raised the instrument to her mouth but the tune had gone utterly out of her head. She lowered the recorder; looked blank and agitated; raised it again – still no tune came. There was an agonising silence until another shepherd came to her rescue and thanked her for a tune none of us had heard. We expected fearful recriminations for this failure: again we were wrong; Christmas was so marvellous its excitement bore her cheerfully along.

Next day Henny, Laura and I climbed the Worcestershire Beacon: we saw the gathering clouds and the brooding misty hills of Hereford and Wales. We were happily luxuriating in our feat of reaching the top, when like an arrow piercing my memory I realized we should be at Stanbrook Abbey for a rehearsal. We ran down the hill; jumped in the car; rushed home; picked up the recorder and the music; raced down for Ross Bowen for he was playing the trumpet. In the great Parlour we were made welcome with trays of tea and bread and butter cut thin as lace. Helena poured out for Ross and me. I then saw another side of Helena: very composed, not at all shy; neither was she precocious – she just played with no mock modesty. They produced the music, not ready before, and at sight she played it faultlessly, stopping only once to ask a question about timing. The nuns were so impressed with both Helena and Ross, they were given more to play than had originally been planned.

24
DAUGHTER OF COMEDY

"Christmas comes but once a year."

Thomas Tusser

Again that Christmas there was a family reunion in the Vicarage. For me it was the Christmas of the red velvet Midis. I had seen these dresses illustrated and advertised in "The Times" – I sent away for them. They arrived all cut out and ready to sew. Mrs Jewell, as good as her name, made them at her cottage in Gilbert's End. The subtle red, the white frilling round the neck, cuffs and hem, made Laura look like a Millais; but not so Helena – she had turned into a Renoir over these last months. They wore these dresses for dinner on Christmas Day and again on Boxing Day, when we gave a party and dance. Henny loved parties with every fibre of her being. Uncle Anthony described her so well on these occasions as "ebullient". I see her still running across the sanded pine floor of the cleared dining room, in her square toed patent leather shoes, making, seizing, willing, enthusing people to dance.

The festivities over, Dawn took Helena and Laura back with her to Kent, to do all the things they had missed the previous year. At first all went well; but then Laura caught 'flu', so on January 1st Willeke caught an early train to Paddington, met Dawn at the station, received a very sick Laura and a very healthy Helena and came back on the next train. Diana and I were busy getting lunch ready when there was a loud cry from the hall, "We're home!" I went to see; and peering through the letter box were two merry, gleaming eyes. A happy Helena pranced in, followed by a strange Laura who walked like a puppet most inexpertly handled.

At the last rehearsal at Stanbrook Abbey the choirs were all present; the entire community was there; and when Helena's turn came she walked to the music stand, very serenely and totally unselfconsciously. She stood there in her blue and tan cape, her fur muff dangling on its cord, her white fur hat on. She looked extraordinarily pretty. Then she played, quite faultlessly, quite unhurriedly, confident, at one with her instrument. It was visually and orally a moment of complete dignity and beauty and it was not her father alone who noted it.

The following Wednesday our older parishioners had their monthly Communion Service and afterwards came to eat mince pies and drink coffee at the Vicarage. We had borrowed an unusual instrument called a Dulcetone from the Jordan family who lived in the village. They had been friendly with "Old Blind George" who had played this bell-like instrument, and the harmonium at St Anne's Well on the Malvern Hills, to the visitors. Again Henny put on her red dress, especially as Mrs Jewell would be present. She played a few tunes. When they had all gone she asked not, "Did I play well?" but "I think they enjoyed it, don't you?"

That ended Christmas and I think I was never so tired in all my life. On the following day I walked up to the cross-roads to catch the bus to Gloucester, uncertain where I should go from there. We docked by a bus going to Bristol so I boarded it. I found the slow journey with its many stops very restful. What a lot we lose by travelling in our own individual wheeled boxes carrying only our own persons and own atmospheres.

At Bristol I went round the "S.S. Great Britain". I ate my sandwiches in a canteen down by the docks. I then climbed up to Clifton. I had hoped to find a hotel in one of the crescents there: I eventually found one in an eighteenth century house, but closer to the main road. From this little hotel I walked and walked amongst people who had no claim upon me – it was quite strange. I was away from the family's noise and demands, yet I thought of Willeke and the girls continuously; but most of all I thought of Helena. I thought of her dignity, then her impetuosity, then her stoniness, then her vivacity. I thought of her shrewdness with money and assets but her incompetence at any kind of maths. I thought of her affectionate nature, but also her "Noli me tangere" quality. Gosh, she was a puzzle. Then, thinking of this one sunny morning as I sauntered down the dark side of Caledonian Place and up the sunny side of the West Mall with its stone mounting blocks, I remembered those words, the only quote in *The Two Gentlemen of Verona:*

> the uncertain glory of an April day,
> which now shows all the beauty of the sun
> And by and by a cloud takes all away.

Significant words, ironical words for my Henny. There was no doubt she had me by the heart-strings; and she was so well named – Helena meant "the bright one" – and truly she was the daughter of comedy. I thought, too, with utter complacency, that it was quite right that I should come so much third in her affections – Mummy first, then Laura, only then me. This followed the family tradition: also mine was a very romantic love and true romantic love has always to have in it an element of the unattainable.

Though Christmas was just over, I browsed in the shops buying a present for each of them at home. For Henny I bought a paper-back of E. Nesbit's "The Railway Children": it was an inspired choice and no book meant more to her and no two days mean more to me than those quite alone in Bristol.

25

UNDERSTANDING, UNDERSTOOD

"Ne'er saw I, never felt, a calm so deep."

William Wordsworth

In March, the Dean of Windsor, Robin Woods, was enthroned as Bishop of Worcester. It was the second occasion of its kind that I had attended and I was interested to see the changes time had brought upon an apparently unchanging ritual. It always does: for though the words may remain the same – even the actions – the spirit around those words and actions alter and our interpretations of them vary. The trumpeters' brash tingling notes crashed along the vaulted aisles; the new Bishop's voice rang out clear and commanding; the Lord Lieutenant's star of the Order of the Garter flashed – were those diamonds real? It was a state occasion. I noticed, though, that we were far less inhibited than formerly: discipline, as we are so often told, has slackened. Clergy and people in the choir moved and grouped more, in order to gain a better view – before we had all been rooted in our places, fearful of moving and thus breaking some grave propriety. As I looked at the clergy with their sideburns and whiskers, I thought, how Victorian we were becoming; and, at times, the whole scene looked like an official painting of a Jubilee, or a royal wedding minus bride and groom.

When, at last, it was all over, I slipped out of the Cloisters and round the cathedral to the Yard where I saw at the top of the steps the small calm figure of Margaret Willetts with her suitcase. Together we watched the Mayor of Worcester, the Corporation, and the assorted mayors of the county leave, then the congregation, all with a look of a new era in their eyes; then came

Willeke, very smart in her brown costume and fur hat.

Diana, Helena and Laura were all at home. Henny had been riding, but had changed into her corduroy dress of blue and green which so suited her. It is a very individual garment, made by Willeke, with long narrow sleeves and floppy pierrot-like cuffs – its pale but glowing colours entirely matched her own glowing pallor. She ran down the steps to greet Margaret: she was rapturous but, somehow, collected. She opened the boot and got out Margaret's case and carried it upstairs. We all had tea and we all talked of our various doings that afternoon. That evening we, the older ones, went to Cheltenham – the excuse for Margaret's visit – to see "Mansfield Park" at the Playhouse.

Sunday arrived and Margaret came to the Family Service, amongst other services, and I noticed a smile hovering over her educationalist face as I paced the aisle asking questions and easing out answers. Helena sat close by her: she was gazing, as she so often did, at the East window and its myriad of colours; but she betrayed no emotion. I wondered what she believed? I wondered what she was thinking of? I recalled saying prayers with her only a week before when she had said, "You know, sometimes, I think Jesus is just another fairy story. Do you?"

"Yes," I agreed. "It is sometimes very difficult to think it is all true."

I did not want to sound dogmatic – I, of all people, had moved through every possible shade of doubt. I continued: "but I am quite certain, now. Jesus did live; he was a real person; and, now, I have no difficulty in believing he rose from the dead." I said no more: she was content with my answer; but for me, ever since my accident, my religion was no longer a matter of Belief but of Knowledge. This knowledge can never be forced upon others, though, and to each it must come in its own way and in its own time. I was quite untroubled about her for she had a tremendous awareness. Only that early Spring I had written a poem about a gate I love in Gloucestershire – some, astoundingly, fail to comprehend it. I read it to Helena and asked her what it was about. With surprise that I should ask an obvious question she had answered, "It is the gate of Death." Margaret did not see a bored child in church, but a mystic, so serene that all emotion left her and she travelled in the spirit to the Spirit. I should have known: for here, once more, she was like me.

Whilst I went to Matins at St Mary's, Margaret returned with the children to the Vicarage. Helena, I'm told, led Margaret to her room and there the two spent an hour looking at her books, her tapestries, her poems, her "I want list", her Spirograph – all her treasures, which she kept so neatly piled on their shelves. Margaret, who knew Henny so well, came to know her even better and their mutual admiration deepened. This was an essential with Henny: to know her you simply had to have her to yourself.

A week later I was in London for the day. In the evening I met Patrick who took me to his palatial club in St James's. We sat in the great window for dinner; and, always, our conversation picked up from where it had been left hours, weeks, months ago – it made no difference. We talked of our wives, our children; and as I was elaborating on the theme of Helena, I saw a bus draw up outside. On the top deck, in the front seat, sat a young man who looked at us. He wondered what we were eating: he wondered, even more, what we were discussing. I looked at myself of twenty five years ago, looking, just as he looked, at the privileged in just such a way, and he imagined, as I had imagined, a conversation, more profound, more wise than is possible amongst most humans. Going home that night in the train I thought of that young man again; and I thought, had he known our conversation at that moment, he would not have been disappointed, for its subject was as beautiful as she was intricate.

There is a gate in Gloucestershire,
in Summer grey-green,
with gay green growth arching around –
the world is well.
When that lane is leafless
then the gate is golden-green:
slanting sun makes the moss glow;
the gate is well –
the world not so.
One day, in God's gated time,
I shall go through that gate
if
I have paid the toll.

26

HOLY DAYS, HOLIDAYS

"But Easter-Day breaks! But
Christ rises! Mercy every way
Is infinite – and who can say?"

Robert Browning

The Railway Children came to the Gaumont cinema in Worcester and on the Monday of Holy Week I took Helena and Laura to an evening performance. They both wore their capes – Willeke had made a tweed poncho-coat for Laura – their muffs and their hats: this was a great occasion. As we waited for the film to end before entering, adults in the foyer smiled at these two, who looked as if they were from the film itself. We sat in the second row of the Upper Circle. The supporting film bored Laura very much indeed and whilst it was showing a couple came in and sat immediately in front of us. The lady unclasped her handbag and took out some sweets; the man lit a cigarette. It was when the second sweet had been unrolled from its crinkly paper and the second cigarette had been lighted that Helena, who sat on the other side of Laura, leant across and whispered very confidentially, but also with some condemnation, tinged with envy, "Those people don't know that it is still Lent." We had all given up sweets.

I whispered back, "No, they don't. But some people might say we shouldn't be in a cinema this week, either."

The lights went up and to my great amusement the couple, who so offended Henny's religious principles, were very well known to us and the husband was a clergyman!

When the big film began then Henny was oblivious of Lent or anything else; and when as the story unrolled the boys, on a paper chase, ran into the tunnel, Laura became frightened and turned to me for comfort. Henny was lost in an Edwardian world. Her face lit with laughter, clouded with concern, wrinkled in sorrow; and she anticipated every episode. When she saw the boys disappear into the tunnel she whispered, "Oh, this is exciting: Bobbie saves them, of course."

Laura, by then, had climbed on to my knee. At the end, when Bobbie meets her father amidst swirls of steam and cries, "Daddy, my Daddy," Helena had so identified herself with Bobbie she seized my hand. The lights came on: to Laura it was a slight relief; Henny sat on. The clergyman and his wife turned to us in a friendly way. Henny ignored them; she emitted no charm; she never even saw, or heard them; she was still in another world. As we walked to the car park she said, "Oh I do wish, I do, do wish, I was as good as Bobbie."

"You will be, my dear. She was older than you, you know."

"Daddy, do please grow a beard like Bobbie's Daddy."

The Distribution of the Royal Maundy was at Tewkesbury Abbey in 1971. Months before I had been to see the poor pestered Vicar there to enquire if there was any hope of a ticket for Diana. Diana had just passed all her qualifications to be a Queen's Guide, so I thought it would be nice for her to see the Queen in the year she became her Guide.

"Well, your request is more modest than one I had this morning. A woman practically demanded sixteen seats for her family and friends and she has nothing to do with the Abbey at all."

We heard nothing from him and I said to Diana that I was afraid there evidently was no hope. On Tuesday, whilst Willeke and I were out, he rang up and told Diana that there were tickets not only for herself but for her parents as well. We were all very excited. We planned to take Helena and Laura and hand them over to the local Brownies lining the path to the Abbey.

Thursday came, a dull day with an absolutely Siberian wind; and Laura was ill. She had a rash and a slight temperature. Helena, with a delight that was most disloyal, elected to stay at home and nurse Laura. We arranged with Jack Kean, a friend who lived across the road, that he would come in and see that all was well. Even before we left, Helena had dug out her old Red Cross uniform, she bustled with thermometers and charts and Laura languished, most appreciatively in all this clinical attention. She played the invalid just as hard as Henny played the nurse.

Whilst we watched the mediaeval pageantry, translated into seventeenth century terms and re-enacted in the twentieth, Helena had turned the Vicarage into a hospital. Each door was labelled Ward 1, 2, 3 and 4. The bathroom was labelled Operating Theatre. When Jack arrived at eleven he was met at the door and told to follow the arrows to Ward 1. He followed the instructions and sat down on Laura's bed and talked to her. He heard the tinkle of cups and in came the Matron bearing a tray laid with coffee and biscuits; but Matron did not smile – she said, "Consultants do not sit on the beds of their patients."

It was after this visit that Jack said to me that he had never realized how intense Helena was: "Not only did she convince me that she was the Matron, but I began to wonder if I was not a doctor after all."

Easter came with all its glorious promises and as if to underline its meaning the weather contrived a "pathetic fallacy". Good Friday, like Thursday, was bitter, grey and cold. It did not deter the children, though, who delightedly built their Easter Garden. Helena arranged flowers quickly and with a lot of variation.

On Saturday the girls and I went down to St Mary's to look at the decorated church. The sun shone; the air was warm. The old church looked lovely and I felt Herrick would have been no end pleased with it. We went out into the churchyard and across the fields to the site of the old castle. We climbed the tump and amongst the silvery grey barked sycamores picked primroses. On our way down Diana kicked an old bird's nest. Helena scurried after it.

"We don't want that", said Diana.

"Oh yes we do," chorussed Helena and I.

Henny immediately put her bunch of primroses in its bowl and back in the churchyard she picked violets which she sprigged all round the edge. It became our table centre.

Sunday dawned even brighter and even warmer and Henny gazing at the East window listened intently as I told the story of the Resurrection. It was the happiest Easter for all our lives.

27
OUTINGS

"The gentleness of heaven is on the Sea:
Listen! the mighty Being is awake
And doth with his eternal motion make
A sound like thunder – everlastingly."

William Wordsworth

Easter Monday was still hotter and in the afternoon, all my sick Communions administered, we walked along the dusty rocky road to Blackmore Camp where a Steam Engine Rally was being held. We had never been to one before, Helena and Laura ran on ahead like two eager little dogs, full of anticipation; all was new; all was unknown. We saw the crowds serpentining round the deserted Nissen huts and broken buildings; and over everything blew billowing clouds of thick almost glutinous smoke; then as we drew still nearer we heard the steam organs.

There were steam engines of every kind: some were slim, well kept, gleaming with brass plates and brass barley sugar columns to support the tin awning over the driver; some were rusty old things, red hot and alarmingly likely to explode. A very fat one looked, I had to admit, like my dear Queen Victoria at her most disagreeable and most ill-dressed – the Queen as seen by Gladstone, no doubt.

"Mummy, look at this one."

"I say, can we climb on that one?"

"Look, the Panton children are having a ride."

"Let's go and hear that organ. Why it's from Holland."

In the heat we drifted slowly around and as the smoke belched I thought how very, very dirty nineteenth century cities must have been. At last we came to a roundabout with the correct ostriches, horses and camels: the little ones could be restrained no more. As they rose and fell, holding on tight to the upright pole, their faces were alight with pleasure. I recognised, however, the moment when Henny's smile became dutiful and mechanical – she felt dizzy and it was a bit boring. On the way home she said, "I'm getting a little too old for roundabouts. I'll never go on another."

It was a busy holiday: swimming at the new swimming pool in Tewkesbury was the craze and often there were pleadings at lunch to Willeke, or me, to take them. There was a party near Kinver which I had to take Helena to. We did not know where the house was, so we had to do some searching: consequently we were late. We drew up before a house and an excited pack of little girls came streaming out of the gate. They were vividly clad in their modern party dresses; but none had a midi, quite as chic as Henny's. A cry went up, "It's Helena. It's Helena." Then I heard murmurings, "What's she wearing?"

Henny, seated by my side, sniffed the admiration in the air; she quivered with excitement; she was a little hound longing to join the pack; she was also the cynosure making an arrival. As I saw her I was hurled back to my childhood, seeing Cinderella, gloriously clad, stepping from her coach fully confident that she is the undoubted centre of the stage. It was a composed, cool, unconceited, but very confident entrance and I had seen its counterpart in a very royal personage in Winchester, years before. Miss Watts, you were so right.

The most important outing of all was to Bristol Zoo. The thrill for both Helena and Laura in this was that neither Willeke nor I had been: they had, with St Mary's School. We arrived about noon and before we had even parked, they had seen a photographer with two green Australian monkeys.

"Oh Mummy, oh Daddy, can't we have our photos taken with them?"

I was tired and hungry, so bad tempered. "Certainly not, it will be ridiculously expensive."

We unpacked the food and still they pleaded and Willeke said, "See how much it costs."

Off they trotted and, far too soon, they returned

with the information.

"Outrageous" I said.

"Go and see if you can both be on one photograph" said temporizing Mummy.

Back they came. The answer was on their faces: they could. Their joy was so abundantly evident that I relented and trailed after them. They squealed with enchantment as the patient, trusting little creatures – mother and son – wearing knitted suits, were placed in their arms.

In the Zoo, all my post-Easter weariness fell away and we followed our zestful children as they flattened their noses gazing through glass panels at boa-constrictors, or leant cautiously over bars looking at white tigers. We saw everything. After a cup of tea they rushed off to see the Sea-lions being fed. When I reached the pool it was one head of curious humanity. I stood on the edge of the crowd wondering where they could be. Suddenly my arm was tapped, it was Henny looking most perturbed, "Daddy, Laura cannot see."

"Bring her to me and I'll put her on my shoulders."

When I had hoisted Laura up, Henny looked relieved and went off to find herself a vantage point.

We were not allowed to leave Bristol without paying our respects to the Suspension Bridge. Anyway I wanted to buy some special tea at Carwardines. Yes, the shops were open; but there was nowhere to park. I got out; ran across the green, beneath the trees whilst Willeke circled around in the car. I was not long and when I came out the grey car was turning down a sharply shadowed little street. Henny and Laura laughed mockingly through the back window as I chased after them; Willeke purposely went a little faster but then let me catch them. Once in I took them round the squares and crescents of that workaday version of Bath, where I had been so content and quiet, thinking of them all, at the New Year. I showed them the hotel where I had stayed, then out to the Suspension Bridge.

The elegant bridge, the dramatic Gorge, Clifton's lovely houses – looking in the sunlight just like some wondrous creation from the imagination of Rex Whistler

– enthralled us all. So much so, that we looked at our watches, it was only four o'clock and in unison we said, "The Sea."

Again excitement, for I had never been to Weston and they were taking me. They knew it well from outings. We parked on the front and they ran immediately to the donkeys. They ambled down the beach and turned and finally gave a lethargic little trot at the end. As Henny jumped down she said, "That's the last time I shall ever go on a donkey."

As they dug sandcastles I went for a walk: I met them later by the pier and we all had high tea. Henny, usually so pale, had cheeks that rayed scarlet like Laura's: they were the embodiment of health and happiness, eating sausages and chips.

There was still one more outing to see my uncle and aunt in Hampshire, whom we had not seen for a long time and never *en masse.* We got up early and set off. The day was an unqualified success and I have a remembrance of Helena in her emerald green velvet dress and lacy white tights organizing games with her cousins in the grounds of the Potter's Heron restaurant. But my main memory of all is of coming home. I was driving and Willeke was sitting in the back with the little ones reading our friend Fred Grice's book, "Severnside Story." She read for two hours – every time she begged for rest we said, "Yes, a short one." We were all so fascinated by this story of Worcester and the county that we urged her on and on until it was finished.

28

THE PARTY

"Fair star of evening, Splendour of the West."

William Wordsworth

School once more. This meant a new straw boater, Miss Gosden with her music again; and this meant something harder. All through the holiday Henny had been practising Beethoven's "Fur Elise". She had always found the angry bit in the middle difficult; she had worked and worked on it and at last could play it without stumbling from beginning to end. "What a surprise for Miss Gosden." She couldn't wait for her lesson. Alas, she had mastered all the notes but at the expense of the timing and the lesson was followed by bitter tears of disappointment – her enterprise had fallen very flat.

On Saturday she went to yet another party, given by a friend whose father was principal of a College of Education. I met Helena in Worcester after the party to bring her home with Vicky Preston. I came upon five ecstatic little girls; but Henny was the most elated of all. They described the hall, the stage, the scenery and curtains, then the equipment in the gymnasium, where the party had been held. Henny's hands curved with delight as she spoke of the ropes and how she had climbed to the top.

"What in your midi?" said a mother.

"Yes, I tucked it up."

And as she said it her face, so delicately boned, so alive with life, radiated. My duckling, never ugly, was becoming a most remarkable swan. I saw that Willeke and I had produced that strange freak, that particular combination of genes, that occurs in every family now and then, that thing which I am old fashioned enough to call "a thoroughbred."

As we came home there was a most vehement sunset over the Malvern Hills.

"Is Mummy at home?"

"Yes."

"Good."

29

THE LIFE CHANGE

"April is the cruellest month."

T.S.Eliot

"But to share with Christ his passion, his crucifixion, His death, means to accept unreservedly all these events in the same spirit as he did."

Archbishop Anthony Bloom

School was over and a small girl climbed on the bus to carry her home. Her older sister was with her, but as usual they went to their separate seats. The smaller girl produced from her pocket a long, ravelled ball of blue string. It would be useful, she thought, perhaps even in the camp she was going to that night with the Guides. She never glanced from the windows as the bus lurched and sped and stopped in the traffic leaving Worcester: instead she turned and twisted her ball of string, trying and trying to find the way to a long fluid harmonious line. The older girl, in a typically sisterly fashion said, "You'll never manage that, it's far too tangled." The girl looked up from the string with a face set in pride with cold grey eyes; her pride was so great she did not answer. Only the very perceptive, or one endowed with a similar pride, would ever know the depth of disdain that glance contained: "Not unravel this string! why, it was the task undertaken and to find and to straighten this long, long line was everything: it was like life, so difficult, intensely absorbing, but intensely perplexing." However, ardour does flag when you are only eleven; the suburban houses gave way to fields; horizons stretched to the Malverns and to Bredon. Here was her village: there was Clive – she waved. The string, not quite half finished, was stuffed into her pocket. The bus gathered speed up the long straight, so thoughts of Camp arose and all the equipment to be laid out and packed. She picked up her satchel; went down the aisle of the bus; the driver smiled at her and pulled up before the gates of her house.

"Thank you, driver."

She ran with a jumble of thoughts: Camp, equipment, but above all, Mummy. All that intense passion quelled caution and she ran to neither Camp, nor Mummy, but into a car and then, unconscious in Mummy's arms, into another world.

Let me not look on blood again,
Nor feel the mindless misery of men.

That morning had been a very busy one, visiting: for Peter Cotton, a friend from Great Witley, was coming for lunch. He had been ordained fairly recently. Over the meal he told us that he had never seen Kempley Church with its unique and lovely wall paintings. We decided to go there. It was a very dull overcast day and as we went down Pell Mell hill near Newent it was dark beneath the trees. I said, though, "We are going to go right past the gate I wrote about in my Easter poem." He slowed up and looked: even on this lightless day he agreed that it had a special quality. I saw it anew, this time in a Samuel Palmer aspect that enhanced it still further in my eyes.

We came to the lonely little church: there were cowslips growing in the churchyard; we went in and walked up to the chancel. I switched on the lights; the colours seemed to drop, move and then glow. I still wished the day had been brighter for Peter though. However, the rich deep ochres vibrated; and I felt that here, I had a vestigial memory of being enclosed within the womb, with similar comforting carmines and warmth all round me. Yes, this was right; indeed it was; for here by the altar one was in the womb of Mother Church. Stretching far back in time and stretching East as well, I encountered in thought and prayer all the Orthodox Church. I remembered Archbishop Anthony Bloom and his saying with such significance from his small and solid frame, "Christ is solid with you to the end."

We had seen all. No, we had seen a great part: such beauty cannot be comprehended in one viewing. We left. In the car our talk was not a continuance of our previous conversation which had been whether in our present age priests should be father-figures? It was more mundane: should we have tea out, or go home? Thank God, we chose to go home.

Tea over, we awaited the arrival of Diana and Helena. We heard the bus draw up, "There it is," said Willeke. Next came the shout of Diana running up the drive "Mummy! Mummy! Mummy!" It was a cry that stilled our blood, but also made us leap to action. It was, incidentally, the last time Diana cried out as a child. Willeke opened the French window and ran out. I ran to the front door, just in case Diana had not seen her mother. We all rushed out: the bus stood still outside our gate; and on the road lay Helena with a halo of blood around her head. I stopped and grasped Laura; Willeke ran forward and let out a cry "O Henny", which in her well-loved voice will ring in my ears for ever and ever. For Willeke, in a moment was not herself alone – she was all suffering motherhood from the beginning of time. She was not even of humankind alone, but the mother in the entire animal world, every age, every kind. I now understand St Paul saying, "the whole Creation groaneth and travaileth in pain together until now."

Peter, later, said, "There was a fearful and poignant moment when the doctor and the mother in Willeke were at war."

Handing Laura over to Peter who went back to the house, I went forward to Willeke. "Get an ambulance." Indoors I dialled 999 and gave faltering directions; I then rang Dr George Lancaster.

Laura came into the hall, as I gathered up a rug she said, "Will Henny die?"

"No", I replied. Oh I did hope that that was true, but I knew it was a false hope.

Out again, Nigel Bowen was kneeling with Willeke propping up Henny's head. I joined them and I tried to pray. As privately I never pray in words, but thoughts and visions, I could only say the Lords prayer, it seemed woefully inadequate. I did beg for her life; but reason in the recesses of my mind also said that it was useless. Suddenly, unlike the steadfast Willeke, I could bear it no longer; it was all too terrible and believe it or no, words from the Duchess of Malfi invaded my mind:

> Cover her face: mine eyes dazzle.
> She died young.

But it was I who covered my face and I turned away. I felt an arm around me: it was a neighbour, Rosie Hurrell, "Come away, Mr Lockwood; come and have some tea."

"No, No."

Then I saw the saloon car and its driver that had run into Helena. The windscreen was shattered; the driver, a man more than middle aged, had blood on his face, I looked again: he was not cut; it was my Henny's blood and a wave of indignation flooded over me.

Cars were going by, and then, suddenly, my immediate predecessor as Vicar of Hanley, Basil Farncombe, came limping forward. He has the charismatic gift of healing. I rushed up to him, grabbed him and pulled the poor lame man to the kneeling group, "Only you can save her." As at the moment before with Laura I disbelieved: but I was willing, though unconvinced, to clutch at straws. Basil, too, knelt.

I rose. I saw another neighbour, Tommy Robertson, emerge from his high hedge and walk up the road; he saw and comprehended all and with the tact that is innate went away.

The ambulance arrived; it turned. "My God, can't it do it quicker than that!" Its doors opened; a stretcher came down. Willeke asked for a coat. There was a momentary hesitation, should I stay with Diana and Laura or go with Henny and Willeke? Of course, I went with Willeke.

The fearful klaxon sounded as soon as we started. We seemed to have gone endless miles. I looked out to see if we were nearing Worcester: we had not covered a mile, we were by Miss Watt's old home. Willeke remained bent over Henny, her arm around her, also feeling her heart; and now and again with a pathetic mixture of mother and doctor she said, "Her heart is still beating, still beating." Again I looked through the window; there was Stanbrook Abbey. On and on we rushed and as we approached Worcester an escort was requested on the inter-com. At the same time I saw the ambulance man begin to massage Henny's chest which was heaving up and down. "Oh dear, dear God, it is nearly, nearly over."

The escort met us and we rushed so fast around the roundabout I thought we should have yet another accident. At the bridge, cleared of traffic, we hit the kerb. We arrived at the Casualty Department and from nowhere Dr George Wilson, another of Willeke's group, materialized. He walked away with Helena on a trolley.

Willeke and I were put into a small room where there was a green upholstered divan and two chairs. I sat on the divan and heard myself say in a social kind of way, "Why don't you sit here, dear? It is so much more comfortable."

"No," said Willeke; but rose immediately adding, "Of course I do. I want to be near you."

We waited, not long. We did not speak. George Wilson entered; a more aghast man I have never seen. He had no need to say anything. We were alone.

Later, "Do you want to see her?"

We ran out towards a curtained cubicle: there was Henny, head in bandages, but now with dark bruised patches beneath her eyes. Willeke and I clung together; but then my grief rose and rose and rose. Like a rocket in the sky, it arched; it burst into a thousand diamond ice-like particles of horror that splintered all over the ground of my being – many are not yet thawed. For the second time, I turned away; a nurse seized me and led me to a stool. I think I sat on it.

We were back in the little room: Willeke wept. We pulled ourselves together and went out to George's car. I sat in the back amidst a jumble of cases and midder-bags. Willy was in front and I put my arms around her neck and she clutched my hands hard. I felt desperately sorry for George: he looked so shaken.

At home the door flew open. Peter, Diana and Laura stood grouped on the steps. Diana's face shone with a bright, false hope. Willy embraced her. I picked up Laura, "Will Henny be alright?". "She has gone to Jesus, my dear."

There were four callers that night and between them they enshrined the noblest and kindest facets of humanity. The first was Basil Farncombe once more. There he stood on his old doorstep shocked and grave, "What is the news?" The particles of ice had formed a floe; I jerked my head back and said, "It is all over."

Basil is so modest a man, with no assumptions, but a divine power dropped a prophet's mantle on his shoulders as he replied, "No, no, no: it is only just beginning." A splendid rebuke.

Suddenly, without any heralding, as we sat disconsolate by the fire, there stood Brigid Flynn, our dear friend and house-help. Brigid is always beautiful with her dark hair and white skin; but there in a white mini-mac, she stood like a wild compassionate Sorrow. Willeke ran to kiss her and together they sat and wept. She came to us every day; she was the best of all our props in those dreadful days.

Diana had all this while taken over the running of affairs; whilst we were at the Infirmary she had informed the Family Planning Clinic that her mother would not be coming. Now, she telephoned all those she thought should be told our news. She answered the door; she let in Dr George Lancaster, the senior partner of the Medical group. On this occasion his round eyes failed to twinkle. A fairly long medical career and an even more amazing war record behind him enabled him to look on undismayed, but not unmoved. He in his time has seen carnage, bestiality, splendour, glory – all has passed. He has a natural gallantry which leaps swiftly to protect all those he loves and, I believe, Willeke is amongst them. He was frustrated: where could he vent his fury on Willeke's behalf? It battered behind his eyelids and then came out, "Sometimes one can only curse the Almighty."

Neither Willeke nor I agreed: it was not God's fault that a little girl ran out from behind a bus and that a driver, may, just may, have been going too fast. We loved George's sympathy and always will; but on his outcry we kept silent.

Another hour passed and the bell rang again. "Not another visitor," I demurred. It was the Archdeacon of Worcester, warm, gentle and kind. He said some prayers. He came as a person; but much much more than a person, he represented, as every priest should, the body of Christ. In him I felt some of the solidity of the rock of Peter. It was the second time that day I had had that feeling, but it seemed a million light years since this afternoon.

So our four visitors were humankind – the beautiful and bountiful response of womanhood; the good man, fundamentally a warrior leaping to defend; the clergy. Here indeed was the heart, the mind and the soul; and in each we found some solace and great strength.

30

THE LONG WEEK

"Here the faithful waver, the faithless fable and miss."

Gerard Manley Hopkins

Friday, at long, long last, dawned: we had awoken all night sobbing. We tried to make the day as ordinary as possible; but it seemed nothing would ever be ordinary again. Diana went off to school; and Mr Broomfield, Laura's headmaster, came to collect her. Alone, we crumpled again: we decided to go to church. We walked up to St Gabriel's and there at the altar rail I said Bishop Brett's prayer, "We give them back to Thee, dear Lord, who gavest them to us ... And Life is Eternal and Love is Immortal and Death is only an Horizon, and an Horizon is nothing save the limit of our sight." It strengthened us both. My fears were taken from me wholly. I knew that I had my answer to the discussion with Peter about the "fatherhood" of priests: I now had to be a father to everyone I encountered and it began with Willeke.

As we walked home she suddenly became acutely distressed. At that moment I was thinking glancingly of Wordsworth and his rapture in the natural world, but deep despair at the loss of his daughter, Dora. I said to Willeke, "Look up to the tops of the trees" – we were in St Gabriel's wood – "see the fresh young green in the sunshine". I discovered then the profound effect a physical stance has. When we looked down our view was bounded by the earth: our thoughts were curtailed; and misery crept in easily. If we looked up, then there was the limitless universe, God and his omniscience.

No sooner home than the Rural Dean and the Vicar of Upton, Charles Hand, and his wife Vera, arrived. They began to arrange the funeral: whilst they were there, Mr Taylor, the undertaker, came. I was discussing matters with him when I saw yet another car pull up and out got Basil Trevor Morgan and his wife Jean, the oldest of my college friends. They, always so busy, had dropped everything to come to us. As Basil entered he said, "I can see that you have let her go." At first I did not know what he was talking about; then I was surprised. I could not prevent her going: to let her go seemed merely rational. Later, I discovered that I tried to retain her, but as one toils through one's sorrow one realizes that to let the departed go is not only the rational thing to do, but must also be the lyrical.

To explain my use of the word lyrical I must return to Birmingham Art Gallery with Helena. We had stood before Ford Madox Brown's picture of an early autumn afternoon. It was all the painstaking care only a Pre-Raphaelite can give to a picture. It is warm; it is clear. The sun shines on the poplars just about to turn: it is a very faithful delineation. I sent a postcard of it to William Plomer and he replied that it was a true picture, a reasonable picture, no more. I thought again, what is missing? I then saw with William's percipient eye that it lacked any spontaneity, any joy, any poetry: it was not lyrical.

Our life became like that: it lacked all lyricism. One worked hard; but not with joy. We had let Helena go, but not spontaneously; and if one is a Christian with a real belief in Heaven, then one can let them go lyrically. There is nothing of greater poetry.

But that Friday I was too busy to think deeply. In the afternoon I had to return to Worcester to identify the body. Tommy Robertson took me; he even went to the mortuary with me as I asked – I had a fear that I might faint again. The sheet was turned back: there was Henny, still wearing her white turban of bandages and, Heaven be blest, not in the least horrifying, but glorious – she looked like a little nun. She was still my beautiful daughter; the dark, bruised patches had gone and her profile was as lovely as ever. I looked rapidly; I gave my assent to a formal question and was prepared to leave, but I could not. I asked to see her once more. Yes, she looked like a nun, utterly chaste. I was deeply comforted.

In the evening I had to go to Stanbrook Abbey to see Dame Hildelith Cumming, the printer – she was making the funeral service sheets for us. As she came in with her usual swift, impetuous stride, she put both hands through the grille and seized mine. Later, too, the Lady Abbess came in; she, too, thrust out her hands and held mine tightly in hers. Both Willeke and I found that this physical contact with others, and with ourselves, meant more than any words.

Next day was quiet; a lull began. It was broken by the delightful surprise of Peter Wardle suddenly appearing: with him we read the two bundles of letters that had arrived as we sat round the kitchen table. Then he left us to go to Bewdley.

In the garden it was still; I was hoeing. Gradually there stole over me an overpowering desire never, never to see another living soul. I worked on but this reaction grew and grew: there has always been a bit of the hermit in me. I could not share this urge with either Willeke, or Diana. It was almost a resolve and then, if I had so decided, the die would surely have been cast. But there was a doubt, ought I to? I flung down my hoe; jumped in the car; and went to Lady Marguerite Lechmere. She answered the door and was astounded to see me. She too stretched out her hands and led me to her sitting room.

When I sat there, I knew why I had come: she would break the spell; she would understand. She, too, many years ago, lost a son aged nineteen. What we said, I do not recall – it did not matter; with those we love it rarely does. We could share our anguish; and looking at her I could see that Willeke and I would survive. Reluctantly I have come to agree with the Black Country woman who, when my mother was dying said, "Now you'll understand what we have to suffer." I still resent her method of statement and the implication that, somehow, at least in her mind, any of us are protected from the ills that fall upon all mankind. I accept her point. Only the most imaginative and the most sensitive can appreciate another's suffering; they are as rare as the genius.

On Sunday, after Holy Communion, Willeke and I chose the place for Henny's grave. She was to be buried. The first reason for this was that Willeke dislikes the protracted rites of a service in church, a long drive to a crematorium and then interment of ashes another day, a prolonged agony.

My reason was that a year before, in an unfamiliar crematorium, I had been very early. The superintendent was both friendly and unoccupied, I questioned him and he began to escort me round. He showed me everything except the *raison d'etre* of a crematorium. "Well", I said, "I've seen everything except the essential." He looked at me smiled and led me to a boiler room where two furnaces roared. Again he viewed me quizzically, "Do you really want to see?" He pushed aside a little metal shield to reveal a spyhole: I looked in. There amidst the curved and cruel flames was a body, blackened, on the wreckage of a coffin like a ship's hulk. The body was a man, skull, chest, stomach and limbs. I was led around to another spyhole at the other end: yes, indeed, a man being systematically burned. It was a most careful and individual destruction. There was no irreverence. But ....

Against it all I set Archbishop Bloom's words, "the body is not a piece of outworn clothing, as some seemingly devout people like to say, which has been cast off by the soul to be free. A body is much more than this for a Christian: there is nothing that befalls the soul in which the body does not take part. We receive impressions of this world, but also of the divine world partly through the body." He speaks, too, of the dignity with which the corpse is revered in the Orthodox Church, as if to expiate for any indignities it may have suffered in life.

This I felt passionately for Helena. She had suffered the awful indignity and outrage of death on the road; her life had been spilled by a mere machine. Machines would play no further part in her destruction. She would be buried with every dignity and handed back to the earth's slow and wonderful cycle.

But before all this, she had to come home. We made

the dining room ready for her. It had always been her room: she adored parties there; she had her piano and her music stand there. Willeke arranged her music: "Fur Elise" was open. Edgar had arrived to tidy the garden, unrequested, and he brought a huge bunch of anemones, brilliant purples and scarlets. Willeke put these in the Easter vases inscribed Jerusalem and Bethlehem. The coffin arrived; we carried it in and placed it on the table. Edgar was hoeing: when he realized the van contained Helena he snatched off his beret, held his hoe like a rifle and stood rigidly to attention, immobile; but his chin quivered.

On the coffin we placed Edgar's anemones and Auntie Liz Godwin's baptismal candlestick. All our raw edges were soothed; her return brought great peace; Willeke slept well for the first time.

31

MORE THAN COMMITTAL

"Sweets to the sweet, farewell."

William Shakespeare

Wednesday came and at 7.30 am Willeke and I were in the little church of Guarlford where the vicar, Hartley Brown, celebrated Holy Communion for us. At long last I found the power of the service and how I hung to the words of the Gospel "A little while and ye shall not see me; and again, a little while and ye shall see me; because I go to the Father." Yes, yes, only a little while, a little while.

As we left the sun came out and it became warm. Later on I went to Stanbrook Abbey to collect the Service sheets. Dame Hildelith had them all ready, beautifully printed in blue with a superb strong Dove of the Holy Spirit, drawn by a novice, on the front. As someone said quite recently that is a dove that does not flutter. I took them to the church: when I entered I was taken aback – it had been transformed into a bower. There were flowers everywhere – and flowers fit for a child. They were so lovingly arranged and it seemed everywhere breathed out sympathy. I saw one of Mr Taylor's men in Helena's grave. He was flowering the turf inside with knots of cherry blossom, cowslips and forget-me-nots. I looked hard at it so that it would not upset me in the afternoon.

At home Willeke and Brigid were cutting sandwiches. It all seemed so desperate we looked into one another's eyes to see if there was some portion of the mind unaffected. No, we exactly mirrored each other's horror and we would draw another deep breath and breathe out through our nostrils. We were so fortunate:

we were lapped in kindness; but it was still all too horrible to be believed.

We dreaded the family's arrival, from Leicester, from Kent and from Southampton: we envisaged ourselves recounting the same story at least three times. By some divinity they all arrived within three minutes of one another. It seemed pre-arranged, but was not; and none of them asked, as we might have guessed, for any details other than we wished to volunteer.

I now felt more sick than I have ever done in my life. I left the family as they tried, so gallantly, to make light-hearted conversation. I had to make my address. I knew that I must, must, must, but could I? I went into the drawing room. I thought I might feel better if I lay down. I stretched myself on the sofa and promptly fainted. As I came round I thought, perhaps, I had better have some fresh air. I went into the garden, I wandered to the bottom and then I fainted off again. I went upstairs to our bedroom and changed into my cassock. I took two talismen, my father-in-law's gold watch and the silver paper clip shaped like a hand that Patrick had given me in Paris. I fainted yet again. Far away I seemed to hear the cars turning in the drive; but I never heard them take Henny from the dining room below. There was a tap on the door; I resolutely steeled myself to see one of my grief-stricken family. But it was Basil Trevor-Morgan. To see someone not closely involved flooded me with strength.

The village seemed to have come to a halt.

At the lych-gate I saw the choir; I saw the clergy; and then Gaston Harward moved out of line. The sun seemed to fall upon him and he grinned at me broadly. How gladly I snatched at that smile, just as I had at P.C. Shuler's almost imperceptible wink to me whilst he had saluted so smartly Henny's coffin.

My aim had been to make Helena's funeral like a wedding and for that reason George Sharp and I had opened the West doors, never opened before in my time; there were now even more flowers – they spilled out of the church. We processed up the aisle.

The Archdeacon of Worcester and the Rural Dean

took the service and Gaston read the lesson in an incisive and compelling way, Hebrews 11 and 12. He began with the challenging question, "What is faith?"

Willeke squeezed my hand, only she and the Rural Dean knew that I had to deliver my sermon. Again I feared that I might faint, or worse, be sick. Holding my talismen I went to the pulpit and preached the words I had written at six in the morning the day before.

"Faith gives substance to our hopes, and makes us certain of realities we do not see."

Our quick-silver daughter is still, but only in this life; she is even quicker in another. All I can say is that we are tremendously grateful to so many people that her life was so happy. In a short time she packed in a great deal and only once – on holiday in Ireland – was she really ill.

She was so gay; David Smith in his letter calls her exuberant; and an honorary uncle, ebullient – both so right. She loved so much and was, whatever it was at that moment, utterly whole-hearted. She made music; she painted; she wrote some interesting bits of poetry; she loved riding; she adored school. The world has lost a lot but God needed her and the time was exactly right.

You see, you must understand Henny was a strong-willed character; and that, sometimes, made life difficult for herself and those around her (but never for her sister Laura). I think she had the seeds of genius within her and geniuses have never been easy to live with. However, she was learning all the time and she had such wonderful teachers every step of the way, so she grew better and better, kinder and nicer. This last Easter holiday was one long delight – the most happy and unclouded month of our married lives and, looking back, filled, not with irony, but completion and fulfilment. It was all spent in Hanley, except for three splendid outings to Bristol Zoo and Weston to my uncle and aunt in Hampshire; and on the last day to Eldersfield to pick cowslips.

Well, that is this world.

Now, the next. Helena, like her mother and her father believed in Christ, the sufferer and the Saviour. But like her father she was a rebellious Christian. This Easter, though, she really and truly believed. And we are glad that on the very day she died, she had had a lesson on the Resurrection, Mary Magdalen, poor old doubting St Thomas, and linking it all with the Spring. Coming home she got off the bus and ran and in her whole-hearted way ran into a better home than ours and more loving arms. But we were with her; she was not with strangers. God had been kind; for what if my quick-silver daughter had survived to be dull and inert?

You kind people, my dear people, you think of our loss. You must not. Helena is forever at the apex of her lively charm and, you know, one day, perhaps in this church, I would have had to hand her over to a bridegroom – and undoubtedly I would have had my reservations – but a bridegroom has chosen her, of whom I cannot possibly disapprove. Also, Henny loved to win – but she matured so much since Christmas that she did not mind losing quite so much. So, because she had learnt that, she has won of the five of us "the race for which we are entered". And I can just see her looking back beaming with pleasure saying "I'm there first."

Faith gives substance to our hopes and makes us certain of realities we do not see. There is a cloud of witnesses of which we, as a family, are so very sure. If we will but look, we see that this world and the next are inextricably mixed. I think of two of Helena's elderly admirers who lived in Hanley Swan, one was Dr Courtney who will grieve for her in Devon; the other is Miss Watts who will welcome her in heaven. She always called Helena "my Princess" and those of you who knew Miss Watts will, with me, have no doubt that, with every propriety and every punctilio observed, she will present our daughter at the Court of God. To Jesus "who for the sake of the joy that lay ahead of him, endured the cross, making light of its disgrace and has taken his seat at the right hand of the throne of God."

The Committal. It was all over and the prayers of my brethren of the Fellowship of Contemplative Prayer in Retreat had supported us.

In sunshine we gave tea to our family and friends. Willeke wandered dazed. She supervised but at a distance. She just really was not there, and she cannot act. Diana followed me and, I think, together we said the right things; but we were acting and as I went back to the kitchen to Brigid and Mrs Lewis, I felt that I went from the stage to the reality of the wings. Most goodbyes made, but by no means all, I went into the kitchen and sat with my two friends. I could bear no more.

Brigid reminded me that as we had sat at coffee a fortnight before, Helena had said, "I should like to know when I am going to die."

"Why?" we had chorussed.

"Well, there'll be a lot to arrange, you know; and I could get all my money out of the bank and spend it."

"Ah, but what if you didn't die and all your money had gone?" we worldly old wise-acres said.

"Oh, I'd just have to start saving again. Anyway, I should have had a very good time."

Next morning and yet another fat wad of letters came and amongst them one from Dr Courtney. He had grieved and very characteristically he had turned his sorrow into his art.

FOR HELENA

Ob. 29.4.71. aged 11.

The flowers along the roadside, as we go
Give beauty, colour, scent upon our way,
When we pass by them gaily day by day.
We pluck them with a careless hand for show,
Nor heed that they will wither and not grow,
Away from parent stem; and in our play,
We think not of their Maker, nor do say,
How thankful we, such happy flowers to know.

Our children are as flowers along life's road.
At times God plucks them with a careful hand
And gives them to his Holy Mother there.
We know not why He needs them so. The load
Of tears is more than we can understand;
Sweet Mary Mother, guard her with thy care.

This subtle sympathy and human perplexity touched us deeply. It had an added and mystical meaning. If Dr Courtney took such pains upon earth, what could not Miss Watts do for her in Heaven? It seemed a miraculous re-assurance, so great that in the afternoon, when the weather broke and I sat in the Coroner's Court listening to my now grown up daughter, Diana, give evidence, I listened with admiration. I watched with some compassion the driver tell his story. Presently it became so repetitive and so meaningless that it was only with tremendous difficulty I kept awake.

32

IMMEDIATE AFTERMATH

"And love is proved in the letting go."

C Day Lewis

"Drop, drop, slow tears" wrote Phineas Fletcher in the seventeenth century; alas, in the latter half of the twentieth century it is almost unseemly to mourn. Permissiveness does not extend to bereavement, or the understanding of mourners. This is, perhaps, the cruellest aspect of our present conventions. One is expected at functions; the show of life must go on, one sometimes wonders why; but one does conform with a smiling face. My cousin Dawn wrote so wisely "the Victorians were right to shut themselves away for a year". I agree with her, as long as such immolation does not nurture bitterness. Then one realizes that such retirement from life is almost impossible, except for the very rich; and it was also in the nineteenth century only the privileged who could withdraw to some retreat. I speak, though, in most general terms: for our friends and our parish were superb examples of Christian understanding; we were very fortunate. There are though many today in the great urban areas who are crippled psychologically because they never come to terms with their sorrow; it is merely buried and shunned.

The worst shock was undoubtedly for Willeke: she had an especial bond with Henny. Willeke's world all but collapsed; she was truly bereft. Returning from the Infirmary she had asked "What do we do now?" A profoundly moving question from one who always has the next step, next stage planned and prepared. For any mother to lose a child is a shattering experience, but it was even magnified in Willeke because she had never experienced death at a close emotional level. Her parents still live; I had lost my mother sixteen years before, so I had had my brush with the wings of Loss.

Diana, as I said in my diary, "was as brave as a lion." We never saw her tears; she concealed them from us. We never saw tears but there were many as she has since told me. She became active and useful; she grew up overnight. The sadness for her was that her relationship with Helena was only just beginning. The age gap had been so great between them; and Helena was so immersed in Laura that time spared for an older sister was severely limited. It was only on the bus going to and from Worcester that anything like a real encounter between them had begun. Even there Helena had always been busy with reading or sewing; no minute had to be wasted. No time had to be wasted on uninteresting subjects either, like mathematics or geography. These she dished out to older children and she collected the finished work before leaving the bus. Life on the bus was well organised.

It was at the bus station that Diana, one day, was hailed by an exultant Helena. Glee and excitement radiated from her face; she seized Diana and dragged her to the waiting room; she pulled so hard two buttons came off her mackintosh. The spectacle that so enraptured Henny was enshrined in three very drunken Irish navvies who were beginning to brawl!

This friendship was nipped, it never was allowed to come to fruition. Helena was proud of Diana. She was looking forward to Diana being made a Queen's Guide. Diana, too, was proud of Helena's achievements. Not least was she proud of her comic spirit and her quick witticisms. Months after Henny's death Diana amused a party of young people at Flatford Mill where she was doing an Ecology course by relating some incident. One girl said, "What fun it must be to have a young sister like that."

"Yes, it is", came the answer.

We were all affected, but Laura's was the hardest to assess for it was masked. She inherits from her great grandfather, a Dutch Lutheran Pastor, an unfailing fount of optimism linked with a quiet reasonableness. Her horror at Henny's death was so acute she rejected it. When the funeral was over, we went to Lyme Regis. The horizons over the sea consoled Willeke, but the sight of the lonely Laura climbing the rails lethargically tore at her heart-strings. She was adrift. She became an even quieter child and buried herself in books; Henny's place was taken by Enid Blyton's "Famous Five", one volume after another.

On our last evening at the hotel Laura talked with a middle-aged woman who was cosily knitting for nearly two hours. When Willeke tucked her up she said, "Mrs Binks says she has a nephew who is a vicar, just like Daddy, and he has two girls, as well. I said to her, but there are three of us. You will tell her about Henny, won't you? I couldn't." Shades of Wordsworth again.

Only now, two years later, does she talk naturally of Helena; and always it is a happy recollection, only slightly wistful. Helena has stamped herself on Laura and sometimes a look, or a sudden vehement annoucement makes one think, for a moment, Helena is there.

I have been the most fortunate of all for I had, after my accident, a true vision of Heaven. So to me it is no distant place, but a living reality. With this privileged knowledge, the most precious of all my possessions, I was able to pick up much of my life, but not the entirety. I found so true the letter of an Anglican nun, an authority on Mysticism, who wrote that losing her sister had been like losing a limb. I was so glad that someone with a great faith could write like that, for it described our feelings exactly.

Another friend had written that "when one is in real trouble, then one realizes that the church is not just an institution but a loving family." It is a loving family, though, without any denominational bounds whatsoever. The falsity of those man-made barriers was revealed so clearly. The Spirit takes no cognisance of such trumpery fences. Hence our help came from Anglicans, Catholics, Methodists and one very special Christian Scientist. It must have been as a result of the prayers of so many that I even had a feeling of exultation. I felt that I would never have any fears again; life could do no more. The apprehensions, however, returned; there have been severe depressions; but slowly one sees life and its details again in time – the details that one previously had loved which in the shock suddenly all disappeared. Poetry helped me and one poet in particular.

In the summer we stayed with Dawn and Don in Kent. We went, one afternoon, to Sissinghurst Castle and wandered round those lovely gardens created by Harold and Vita Nicolson. With blank hearts we rather perfunctorily viewed the flowers and still more limply imagined the Nicolson menage. Then I remembered seeing a letter from Richard Church in The Times and I thought I recalled that his address had been Sissinghurst Castle. Some years before I had met him after a lecture in Worcester and spent a couple of very happy hours in his company. With tremendous hesitancy I went to his door. I knocked; he answered – he looked unchanged, the same endearing wizard, who had got entangled with the Civil Service at a formative period of his life. He did not remember me; I had not expected that he would. Furthermore, he was disappointed that it was me, as he was expecting his son from the Lebanon with his family. A table behind him was ceremonially set with silver and glass for a dinner party. Yet, in spite of all this, our spirits met, blazed and we leapt from topic to topic and suddenly, most unexpectedly I found myself telling him about Henny. He looked at me with his infinitely wise, tragically experienced eyes and said,

"Grief is a sickness of the soul."

It was as though he were a spiritual surgeon; for he wielded those words like a scalpel that sharply and accurately outlined the tumour of my misery and then most neatly excised it.

I admired Richard Church; but those words to me are his greatest. Yes, indeed, a wizard in a velvet jacket and a tidy bow tie.

This sudden relief made me more aware of Willeke's grief. She had to wait more months to meet her equivalent of Richard Church. It was at a party and she met a woman, who some ten years before had lost her son in a car accident, just after he had taken his

Finals at Cambridge. Willeke asked "Does the pain ever get any less?" The gentle brown eyes in an even gentler face answered most truthfully.

"No. It gets no better; but it does come less often."

Willeke accepted that and waited. Her very logical Dutch mind works from point to point until the whole matter is comprehended and digested. That is how she tackles all intellectual questions: so it was with the emotional problems of bereavement. I grasp and grab at truths revealed in lightning flashes of intuition; but there are infinite cavities of ignorance. Willeke is much more reasonable; a firmer more dependable being. So it was that while Willeke toiled unhappily on but always uphill, I danced in strange ecstasies only to fall into depths. But we have always been able to support one another.

We did, jointly, make one mistake. One which, I suppose, many unhappy people make. We tended to divide our friends and acquaintances into two sharp categories, those who reacted sympathetically and those who had not. Only after more than a year did we realize what we were doing and recalled St. Paul's words that all do not have the same gifts. There were many decent, intelligent and useful citizens who perhaps lacked the ability to show their sympathy. We judged them, which we should not have done: they still needed our appreciation, even our love – we had become narrow, even rather selfish.

I worked out a theory that for the Christian the word 'tragedy' has no meaning, for ultimately we always have our belief in the Victory in another life. To be aware of this constantly is very difficult. Only now do I realize why it is I have to preach of the same things so often – because we all forget. There is, though, a physical factor linked with my unhappiness. I must never become overtired: then I fall prey to depression and unwillingly, especially if I am in a moving vehicle, I relive every moment of Helena's death second by second. It is all so sharply focussed in my memory and it unrolls like a film, not a series of stills: but strangely it does have one consolation, Helena looks graceful in attitude and her face is untouched.

This, I know, is merely the material and cannot compare with the glory she enjoys – a glory I saw in a dream, if it was a dream, when I saw her driving a pony and trap, racing by with a look of intense triumph, just as happy as could be. That was a solace and one Willeke envied. Then another day I returned from an interminable meeting in Worcester. Willeke was out, I took out my stew from the oven, placed it on the table and switched on the radio. The kitchen was filled with Faure's Requiem. As it worked through to "In Paradisum" so again a rocket climbed in my soul, up and up and up, again it burst – this time with Joy. It was an echo of the heavenly choirs; and Henny, my Henny, was singing just like that.

It was Heaven and Heaven is always so unexpected.

33

PARTIAL ANSWERS

"Prayer is the peace of our spirit, the stillness of our thoughts, the evenness of our recollection, the seat of our cares, and the calm of our tempests; prayer is the issue of a quiet mind, of untroubled thoughts. It is the daughter of charity and the sister of meekness."

Jeremy Taylor

The pagan in one asks "Why?" The wise man never asks – the whole of life and the world is full of unanswered questions. There was in Helena so much promise and it seemed broken. In my bad moments I mourn certainly not for Helena, nor myself, but for the world, for she had so much to give, something unique. Hence this book.

I do not have to be told that there have been greater catastrophes, worse bereavements after long and debilitating illnesses filled, even in young lives, with pain and despair: I have seen them myself. But each life is unique and this great and potent value is being forgotten as Western civilisation becomes daily more dully identical. To combat this direful monotony we must acknowledge and realize the glorious individuality of each soul. Asserting this, then, Helena's small life was unique.

Is it only hindsight that makes me see a pattern in the whole of her life and mine? Was so much of my life a preparation for the terrible event? It seems odd to me that after I left school I ceased to write poetry – the vein was unmined for six years – then I saw a small boy killed by a lorry. The shock reopened the entrance to that shaft of words.

Then there was a scene in the Common Room of my theological college. We were having a course in Communication. Sprawled along a window-sill was a very clever double-first, but he was also very callow. He baited another clever man with "How can you explain the reason to a mother when her child is dying in a street accident?" The intellectual began talking of forces and impacts and inevitability. My heart congealed in horror as they argued: for neither made an attempt to imagine the scene – they were so blind. It was then that I decided that try as it might cold theology will always fail to explain the inexplicable. Poetry does it one better for it rarely tries to find a full answer. I am content to quote Hardy's poem "The Convergence of the Twain" which he wrote on the sinking of the Titanic.

> Alien they seemed to be;
> No mortal eye could see
> The intimate welding of their later history.

Helena running; the car rushing.

But there is more to explain than just the collision of glass and metal and a girl of eleven. Over those years there had been a strange and remarkable development. Given time, what would she have become? On that last Easter Eve, when we had walked over the tump of Hanley Castle and picked up the bird's nest, we had called on a parishioner for a cup of tea. I saw Margaret look searchingly at Henny. I said nothing, but a few days later she volunteered the information, "I should never worry about Helena, she'll certainly be a something, or a someone. I don't know what. She could be a novelist, or an artist, or a very notable drop-out. But she will always be something."

I remember Miss Phillips' words, too, "As you know she was keen on music and worked hard, but especially in singing when she could appreciate the words." Words would, I think, have taken over from music: there are signs of this in her poem "The Owl" which appeared in the Alice Ottley School Magazine.

This awakening mind was accompanied by an emotional relaxation; she knew fully, at last, that she was loved and so she was more loving. In the strange flickering pattern of our relationship I find strangest of all, that on the day she died, she climbed up into our bed, snuggled up to me warm and sleepy and for the first time, and the last, she was not a "Bag of golf clubs". I am so glad I told her so. Was that coincidence?

But now the echoing void. We missed her in everything, but especially her voice and most particularly the prolonged "Dough" – a constant utterance in moments of irritation. We missed her screwed up nose when something made her squeamish. We missed, oh how we missed, those manifold activities – the rushing up and down of front and back stairs, the flurry into the garden. Two years later we still miss most of all her abiding enthusiasm: it was a spring that never failed.

"What sort of a day have you had?"

"Oh a LOVELY one" was nearly always the reply.

Poor Willeke had to finish making a skirt and a waistcoat of purple and blue tweed that Henny had chosen but would never wear. My bad moment was when I saw that her economy had stretched beyond the grave. She most heartily disapproved of messy farmers who litter fields with empty fertilizer bags and other superfluities. On one walk she had reprovingly gathered up the orange plastic twine she found on the grass and in the hedges. In the vegetable garden I found Edgar had used them to tie up the bean poles. Henny had said,"This will come in very useful."

I longed for her at Evensong on Sundays. She usually sat by me wearing her robes. Often, more often than I care to admit, I would glance at her beautifully balanced profile, upright forehead, straight little nose and ear, all set in perfect juxtaposition with her eyes and her mouth. Each feature was good and what is more unusual in absolute harmony with every other. Two months after her death I was in Malvern Public Library. I idly picked up Harold Kurtz's biography of the Empress Eugenie. The book fell open at Winterhalter's portrait of her in profile. For a moment I was dazzled; I even felt a freezing to my marrow: for though it was the portrait of a mature woman, it was also in its perfection the profile of Helena.

I took the book home: it was not very perceptive; but it did give an outline of her character – a most loving sister, a most loving mother, a very loyal wife; ambitious, religious, a superb hostess; at time marmoreal, at others vivacious, capricious, pure woman. Helena was so much of this. The Empress, when dead, was clothed in the habit of a nun, "It was not inappropriate that on the threshold of eternity she should, for she had overcome the world and founded her own discipline."

I thought of the Henny I last saw in the Infirmary, with her bandaged head, a little nun. There was there the calm, the purpose, the joy of creation, the selflessness – all that I had seen when she made music at Stanbrook Abbey. There had been that special lyricism.

I am almost tempted to think that the Empress smiling at me in the Royal Hotel in Scarborough was seeking, through me, an escape from some limbo in order to "redeem the time." Then a Christian belief and a very natural pride forbid me to think that Henny's soul was in any way second-hand, albeit beautiful, albeit exalted. No, I believe that Henny's virtues and Henny's faults remarkably corresponded with those of the Empress; but it was decreed by the Director of her days that she did not have to grope her way over ninety wretched human years to fit her for Heaven – she was ready at eleven.

There are three sayings of three wise women that Willeke and I find more than helpful. The first was from Lady Marguerite Lechmere, "Your Helena was a mature soul"

The second was from Margaret Willetts, "So many children have been through my hands and I could always see what they would be like when grown up. I could never do this with Helena. It puzzled me: now I know why."

The third was the Lady Abbess of Stanbrook Abbey, "Helena died in the full glory of her baptismal vows, a pure woman."

Pure woman; a pure woman. True, true, true.

So many of my wishes had come true: she had been like a wood anemone, pale, definite in outline, graceful – even in death.

John Hencher with his customary percipience wrote after visiting us that he had been happy with us because we had let him share not in the memory of Helena but in her reality. Helena was so real that she can never, never, be a mere memory: she is far too vital for that. So she is still a member of our family and still living.